Hands-On Full Stack Development with Spring Boot 2.0 and React

Build modern and scalable full stack applications using the Java-based Spring Framework 5.0 and React

Juha Hinkula

BIRMINGHAM - MUMBAI

Hands-On Full Stack Development with Spring Boot 2.0 and React

Commissioning Editor: Richa Tripathi
Acquisition Editor: Shriram Shekhar
Content Development Editor: Akshada Iyer
Technical Editor: Abhishek Sharma
Copy Editor: Safis Editing
Project Coordinator: Prajakta Naik
Proofreader: Safis Editing
Indexer: Pratik Shirodkar
Graphics: Jisha Chirayil
Production Coordinator: Shantanu Zagade

First published: June 2018

Production reference: 1190618

Published by Packt Publishing Ltd.
Livery Place
35 Livery Street
Birmingham
B3 2PB, UK.

ISBN 978-1-78913-808-5

www.packtpub.com

To my wife, Pirre, and daughter, Anni, for their support and the time that I was able to spend with this project. To Mrs Riitta Blomster, for proofreading some difficult parts during the project. To all my motivated students, for inspiring me to continue the lifelong journey of learning.

`mapt.io`

Mapt is an online digital library that gives you full access to over 5,000 books and videos, as well as industry leading tools to help you plan your personal development and advance your career. For more information, please visit our website.

Why subscribe?

- Spend less time learning and more time coding with practical eBooks and Videos from over 4,000 industry professionals

- Improve your learning with Skill Plans built especially for you

- Get a free eBook or video every month

- Mapt is fully searchable

- Copy and paste, print, and bookmark content

PacktPub.com

Did you know that Packt offers eBook versions of every book published, with PDF and ePub files available? You can upgrade to the eBook version at `www.PacktPub.com` and as a print book customer, you are entitled to a discount on the eBook copy. Get in touch with us at `service@packtpub.com` for more details.

At `www.PacktPub.com`, you can also read a collection of free technical articles, sign up for a range of free newsletters, and receive exclusive discounts and offers on Packt books and eBooks.

Contributors

About the author

Juha Hinkula is a software development lecturer at Haaga-Helia University of Applied Sciences in Finland. He received an MSc degree in computer science from the University of Helsinki. He has over 15 years of industry experience in software development. Over the past few years, he has focused on modern full stack development. He is also a passionate mobile developer with Android native technology and nowadays also uses React Native.

About the reviewer

Biharck Araújo has been working as a main software architect and lead programmer for the past 15 years. He is passionate about technology and academic research. He has been working with JavaEE technology for web projects that demanded high-security standards for information transmission for companies of different sectors. He has a vast experience in activities regarding software architecture. He is currently a PhD student at UFMG. He works in bioinformatics using technology in life's favor.

Packt is searching for authors like you

If you're interested in becoming an author for Packt, please visit authors.packtpub.com and apply today. We have worked with thousands of developers and tech professionals, just like you, to help them share their insight with the global tech community. You can make a general application, apply for a specific hot topic that we are recruiting an author for, or submit your own idea.

Table of Contents

Preface   1

Chapter 1: Setting Up the Environment and Tools – Backend   7
  Technical requirements   7
  Setting up the environment and tools   7
    Installing Eclipse   8
    The basics of Eclipse and Maven   8
    Creating the project with Spring Initializr   10
    How to run the project   12
    Spring Boot development tools   18
    Logs and problem solving   18
    Installing MariaDB   21
  Summary   23
  Questions   24
  Further reading   24

Chapter 2: Using JPA to Create and Access a Database   25
  Technical requirements   25
    Basics of ORM, JPA, and Hibernate   26
    Creating the entity classes   26
    Creating CRUD repositories   34
    Relationships between tables   40
    Setting up the MariaDB database   48
  Summary   50
  Questions   51
  Further reading   51

Chapter 3: Creating a RESTful Web Service with Spring Boot   53
  Technical requirements   53
  Creating a RESTful web service with Spring Boot   53
    Basics of REST   54
    Creating a RESTful web service   55
    Using Spring Data REST   61
  Summary   68
  Questions   68
  Further reading   69

Chapter 4: Securing and Testing Your Backend   71
  Technical requirements   71
    Spring Security   71

Securing your backend using JWT   82
Testing in Spring Boot   91
Creating unit tests   92
Summary   96
Questions   96
Further reading   97

Chapter 5: Setting Up the Environment and Tools – Frontend   99
Technical requirements   99
Installing Node.js   100
Installing VS Code   101
Creating and running a React app   103
Modifying a React app   105
Summary   107
Questions   108
Further reading   108

Chapter 6: Getting Started with React   109
Technical requirements   109
Basic React components   109
Basics of ES6   114
Understanding constants   114
Arrow functions   115
Template literals   116
Classes and inheritance   116
JSX and styling   117
Props and state   118
Component life cycle methods   121
Handling lists with React   122
Handling events with React   124
Handling forms with React   125
Summary   128
Questions   129
Further reading   129

Chapter 7: Consuming the REST API with React   131
Technical requirements   131
Using promises   131
Using the Fetch API   133
Practical examples   135
Summary   144
Questions   145
Further reading   145

Chapter 8: Useful Third-Party Components for React   147
Technical requirements   147

Using third-party React components 148
React Table 153
The modal window component 158
Material UI component library 162
Routing 165
Summary 169
Questions 169
Further reading 169

Chapter 9: Setting Up the Frontend for Our Spring Boot RESTful Web Service 171
Technical requirements 171
Mocking up the user interface 172
Preparing the Spring Boot backend 173
Creating the React project for the frontend 175
Summary 177
Questions 177
Further reading 177

Chapter 10: Adding CRUD Functionalities 179
Technical requirements 179
Creating the list page 179
The delete functionality 186
The add functionality 193
The edit functionality 198
Other functionalities 203
Summary 205
Questions 205
Further reading 205

Chapter 11: Styling the Frontend with React Material-UI 207
Technical requirements 207
Using the Button component 208
Using the Grid component 211
Using the TextField components 212
Using the AppBar component 214
Using the SnackBar component 216
Summary 218
Questions 219
Further reading 219

Chapter 12: Testing Your Frontend 221
Technical requirements 221
Using Jest 222
Snapshot testing 224
Using Enzyme 227

Summary 229
Questions 229
Further reading 230

Chapter 13: Securing Your Application 231
Technical requirements 231
Securing the backend 232
Securing the frontend 233
Summary 244
Questions 245
Further reading 245

Chapter 14: Deploying Your Application 247
Technical requirements 247
Deploying the backend 248
Deploying the frontend 256
Using Docker containers 258
Summary 263
Questions 264
Further reading 264

Chapter 15: Best Practices 265
What to learn next 265
HTML 266
CSS 266
HTTP 266
JavaScript 266
A backend programming language 266
Some frontend libraries or frameworks 267
Databases 267
Version control 267
Useful tools 267
Security 267
Best practices 268
Coding conventions 268
Choosing the proper tools 268
Choosing the proper technologies 269
Minimizing the amount of coding 269
Summary 269
Questions 270
Further reading 270

Assessments 271

Other Books You May Enjoy 281

Index 285

Preface

In this book, we will create a modern web application using Spring Boot 2.0 and React. We will start from the backend and develop a RESTful web service using Spring Boot and MariaDB. We will also secure the backend and create unit tests for it. The frontend will be developed using the React JavaScript library. Different third-party React components will be used to make the frontend more user friendly. Finally, the application will be deployed to Heroku. The book also demonstrates how to Dockerize our backend.

Who this book is for

This book is written for:

- Frontend developers who want to learn full stack development
- Backend developers who want to learn full stack development
- Full stack developers who have used some other technologies
- Java developers who are familiar with Spring, but haven't ever built a full-stack application.

What this book covers

Chapter 1, *Setting Up the Environment and Tools – Backend*, explains how to install the software needed for backend development and how to create your first Spring Boot application.

Chapter 2, *Using JPA to Create and Access a Database*, introduces JPA and explains how to create and access databases with Spring Boot.

Chapter 3, *Creating a RESTful Web Service with Spring Boot*, shows how to create RESTful Web Services using Spring Data REST.

Chapter 4, *Securing and Testing Your Backend*, explains how to secure your backend using Spring Security and JWT.

Chapter 5, *Setting Up the Environment and Tools – Frontend*, explains how to install the software needed for frontend development.

Chapter 6, *Getting Started with React*, introduces the basics of the React library.

Chapter 7, *Consuming the REST API with React*, shows how to use REST APIs with React using the Fetch API.

Chapter 8, *Useful Third-Party Components for React*, demonstrates some handy components that we'll use in our frontend development.

Chapter 9, *Setting Up the Frontend for Our Spring Boot RESTful Web Service*, explains how to set up the React app and Spring Boot backend for frontend development.

Chapter 10, *Adding CRUD Functionalities*, shows how to implement CRUD functionalities to the React frontend.

Chapter 11, *Styling the Frontend with React Material-UI*, shows how to polish the user interface using the React Material-UI component library.

Chapter 12, *Testing Your Frontend*, explains the basics of React frontend testing.

Chapter 13, *Securing Your Application*, explains how to secure the frontend using JWT.

Chapter 14, *Deploying Your Application*, demonstrates how to deploy an application to Heroku and how to use Docker containers.

Chapter 15, *Best Practices*, explains the basic technologies that are needed to become a full stack developer and covers some basic best practices for software development.

To get the most out of this book

The reader should possess the following:

- Basic knowledge of using some terminal such as PowerShell
- Basic knowledge of Java and JavaScript programming
- Basic knowledge of SQL databases
- Basic knowledge of HTML and CSS

Download the example code files

You can download the example code files for this book from your account at www.packtpub.com. If you purchased this book elsewhere, you can visit www.packtpub.com/support and register to have the files emailed directly to you.

You can download the code files by following these steps:

1. Log in or register at `www.packtpub.com`.
2. Select the **SUPPORT** tab.
3. Click on **Code Downloads & Errata**.
4. Enter the name of the book in the **Search** box and follow the onscreen instructions.

Once the file is downloaded, please make sure that you unzip or extract the folder using the latest version of:

- WinRAR/7-Zip for Windows
- Zipeg/iZip/UnRarX for Mac
- 7-Zip/PeaZip for Linux

The code bundle for the book is also hosted on GitHub at `https://github.com/PacktPublishing/Hands-On-Full-Stack-Development-with-Spring-Boot-2.0-and-React`. In case there's an update to the code, it will be updated on the existing GitHub repository.

We also have other code bundles from our rich catalog of books and videos available at `https://github.com/PacktPublishing/`. Check them out!

Conventions used

There are a number of text conventions used throughout this book.

`CodeInText`: Indicates code words in text, database table names, folder names, filenames, file extensions, pathnames, dummy URLs, user input, and Twitter handles. Here is an example: "Create a new class called `CarRepository` in the `domain` package."

A block of code is set as follows:

```
@Entity
public class Car {

}
```

Any command-line input or output is written as follows:

```
mvn clean install
```

Bold: Indicates a new term, an important word, or words that you see onscreen. For example, words in menus or dialog boxes appear in the text like this. Here is an example: "Activate the root package in the Eclipse **Project Explorer** and right-click. Select **New | Package** from the menu."

 Warnings or important notes appear like this.

 Tips and tricks appear like this.

Get in touch

Feedback from our readers is always welcome.

General feedback: Email `feedback@packtpub.com` and mention the book title in the subject of your message. If you have questions about any aspect of this book, please email us at `questions@packtpub.com`.

Errata: Although we have taken every care to ensure the accuracy of our content, mistakes do happen. If you have found a mistake in this book, we would be grateful if you would report this to us. Please visit `www.packtpub.com/submit-errata`, selecting your book, clicking on the Errata Submission Form link, and entering the details.

Piracy: If you come across any illegal copies of our works in any form on the Internet, we would be grateful if you would provide us with the location address or website name. Please contact us at `copyright@packtpub.com` with a link to the material.

If you are interested in becoming an author: If there is a topic that you have expertise in and you are interested in either writing or contributing to a book, please visit `authors.packtpub.com`.

Reviews

Please leave a review. Once you have read and used this book, why not leave a review on the site that you purchased it from? Potential readers can then see and use your unbiased opinion to make purchase decisions, we at Packt can understand what you think about our products, and our authors can see your feedback on their book. Thank you!

For more information about Packt, please visit packtpub.com.

Setting Up the Environment and Tools – Backend

1

In this chapter, we will set up the environment and tools needed for backend programming with Spring Boot. Spring Boot is a modern Java-based backend framework that makes development faster than traditional Java-based frameworks. With Spring Boot, you can make a standalone web application that has an embedded application server.

In this chapter, we will look into the following:

- Building the environment for Spring Boot development
- The basics of Eclipse IDE and Maven
- Creating and running Spring Boot projects
- Solving common problems of running Spring Boot applications

Technical requirements

Java SDK version 8 or higher is necessary to use of Eclipse IDE.

In this book, we are using the Windows operating system, but all tools are available for Linux and macOS as well.

Setting up the environment and tools

There are a lot of different IDE tools that you can use to develop Spring Boot applications. In this book, we are using Eclipse, that is an open source IDE for multiple programming languages. We will create our first Spring Boot project by using the Spring Initializr project starter page. The project is then imported into Eclipse and executed. Reading the console log is a crucial skill when developing Spring Boot applications.

Installing Eclipse

Eclipse is an open source programming IDE developed by the Eclipse Foundation. An installation package can be downloaded from `https://www.eclipse.org/downloads`. Eclipse is available for Windows, Linux, and macOS. You should download the latest version of Eclipse IDE for Java EE developers.

You can either download a ZIP package of Eclipse or an installer package that executes the installation wizard. If using the ZIP package, you just have to extract the package to your local disk and it will contain an executable `Eclipse.exe` file, that you can run by double-clicking on the file.

The basics of Eclipse and Maven

Eclipse is an IDE for multiple programming languages, such as Java, C++, and Python. Eclipse contains different perspectives for your needs. A perspective is a set of views and editors in the Eclipse Workbench. The following screenshot shows common perspectives for Java development:

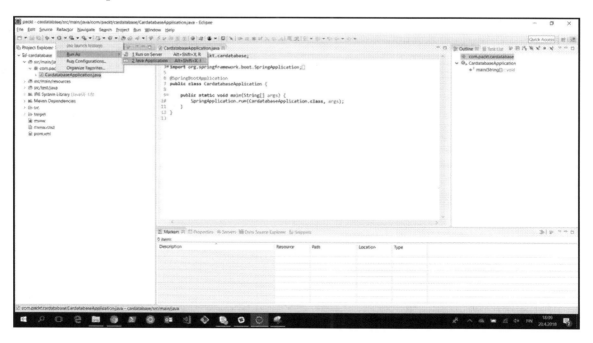

On the left side, we have **Project Explorer**, where we can see our project structure and resources. **Project Explorer** is also used to open files by double-clicking on them. The files will be opened in the editor, that is located in the middle of the workbench. The **Console** view can be found in the lower section of the workbench. The **Console** view is really important because it shows application logging messages.

You can get the **Spring Tool Suite (STS)** for Eclipse if you want, but we are not going to use it in this book because the plain Eclipse installation is enough for our purposes. STS is a set of plugins that makes Spring application development easier (https://spring.io/tools).

Apache Maven is a software project management tool. The basis of Maven is the **project object model (pom)**. Maven makes the software development process easier and it also unifies the development process. You can also use another project management tool called Gradle with Spring Boot, but in this book, we will focus on using Maven.

The pom is a `pom.xml` file that contains basic information about the project. There are also all the dependencies that Maven should download to be able to build the project.

Basic information about the project can be found at the beginning of the `pom.xml` file, which defines, for example, the version of the application, packaging format, and so on.

The minimum version of the `pom.xml` file should contain the project root, `modelVersion`, `groupId`, `artifactId`, and `version`.

Dependencies are defined inside the dependencies section, as follows:

```
<?xml version="1.0" encoding="UTF-8"?>
<project xmlns="http://maven.apache.org/POM/4.0.0"
xmlns:xsi="http://www.w3.org/2001/XMLSchema-instance"
  xsi:schemaLocation="http://maven.apache.org/POM/4.0.0
http://maven.apache.org/xsd/maven-4.0.0.xsd">
  <modelVersion>4.0.0</modelVersion>

  <groupId>com.packt</groupId>
  <artifactId>cardatabase</artifactId>
  <version>0.0.1-SNAPSHOT</version>
  <packaging>jar</packaging>

  <name>cardatabase</name>
  <description>Demo project for Spring Boot</description>
```

```
<parent>
  <groupId>org.springframework.boot</groupId>
  <artifactId>spring-boot-starter-parent</artifactId>
  <version>2.0.1.RELEASE</version>
  <relativePath/> <!-- lookup parent from repository -->
</parent>

<dependencies>
  <dependency>
    <groupId>org.springframework.boot</groupId>
    <artifactId>spring-boot-starter-web</artifactId>
  </dependency>

  <dependency>
    <groupId>org.springframework.boot</groupId>
    <artifactId>spring-boot-starter-test</artifactId>
    <scope>test</scope>
  </dependency>
</dependencies>
</project>
```

Maven is normally used from the command line. Eclipse contains embedded Maven, and that handles all the Maven operations we need. Therefore, we are not focusing on Maven command-line usage here. The most important thing is to understand the structure of the pom.xml file and how to add new dependencies to it.

Creating the project with Spring Initializr

We will create our backend project with Spring Intializr, that is a web-based tool that's used to create Spring Boot projects. Spring Intializr can be found at https://start.spring.io:

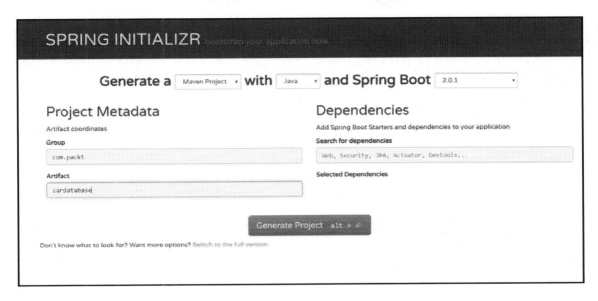

We will generate a Maven project with Java and the latest Spring Boot version. In the **Group** field, we will define our group ID, that will also become a base package in our Java project. In the **Artifact** field, we will define the artifact ID, that will also be the name of our project in Eclipse.

In the **Dependencies** section, we will select the starters and dependencies that are needed in our project. Spring Boot provides starter packages that simplify your Maven configuration. Spring Boot starters are actually a set of dependencies that you can include in your project. You can either type the keyword of the dependency into the search field, or you can see all available dependencies by clicking on the **Switch to the full version** link. We will start our project by selecting two dependencies—**Web** and **DevTools**. You can type the dependencies into the search field or switch to the full version and see all the starter packages and dependencies available:

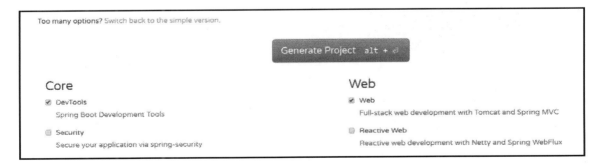

The **DevTools** dependency provides us with Spring Boot development tools, that provide automatic restart functionality. It makes development much faster because the application is automatically restarted when changes have been saved. The web starter pack is a base for full-stack development and provides embedded Tomcat.

Finally, you have to press the **Generate Project** button and that generates the project starter ZIP package for us.

How to run the project

1. Extract the project ZIP package that we created in the previous topic and open Eclipse.
2. We are going to import our project into Eclipse IDE. To start the import process, select the **File | Import** menu and the import wizard will be opened. The following screenshot shows the first page of the wizard:

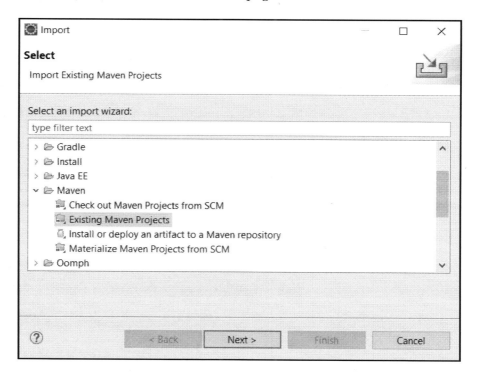

3. In the first phase, you should select **Existing Maven Projects** from the list under the Maven folder, and then go to the next phase by pressing the **Next** button. The following screenshot shows the second step of the import wizard:

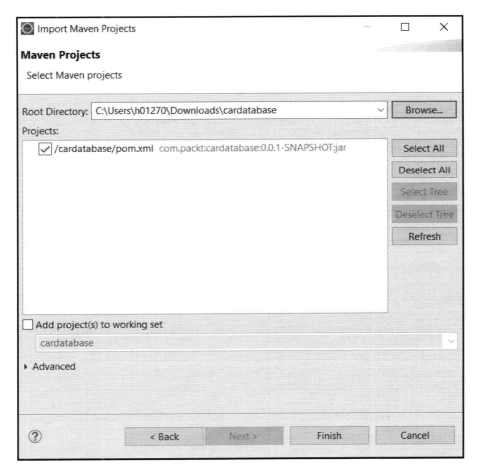

4. In this phase, select the extracted project folder by pressing the **Browse...** button. Then, Eclipse finds the pom.xml file from the root of your project folder and shows it inside the **Projects** section of the window.

5. Press the **Finish** button to finalize the import. If everything went correctly, you should see the `cardatabase` project in Eclipse **Project Explorer**. It takes a while when the project is ready because all dependencies will be loaded by Maven after import. You can see the progress of the dependency download at the bottom-right corner of Eclipse. The following screenshot shows Eclipse **Project Explorer** after successful import:

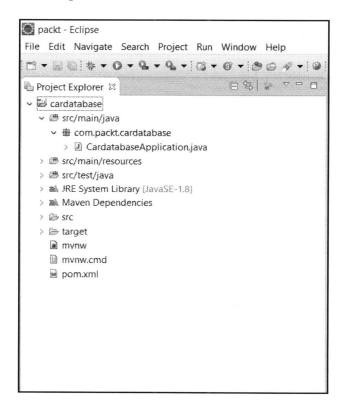

The **Project Explorer** also shows the package structure of our project, and now at the beginning there is only one package called `com.packt.cardatabase`. Under that package is our main application class, called `CardatabaseApplication.java`.

6. Now, we don't have any functionality in our application, but we can run it and see whether everything has started successfully. To run the project, open the main class by double-clicking on it and then pressing the **Run** button in the Eclipse toolbar, or select the run menu and press **Run as | Java Application**:

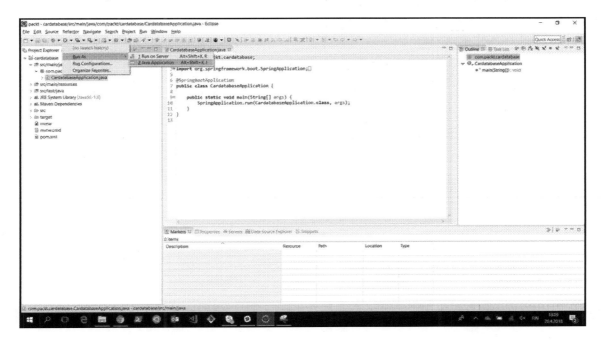

You can see the **Console** view opening in Eclipse, and that contains important information about the execution of the project. This is the view where all log texts and error messages appear, and it is therefore really important to check the content of the view when something goes wrong.

Now, if the project was executed correctly, you should see the text `Started`
`CardatabaseApplication in...` at the end of the console. The following screenshot
shows the content of the Eclipse console after our Spring Boot project has been started:

```
  /\\ /___'_ _ _ _(_)_ __ __ _ \ \ \ \
 ( ( )\___ | '_ | '_| | '_ \/ _` | \ \ \ \
  \\/  ___)| |_)| | | | | || (_| |  ) ) ) )
  '  |____| .__|_| |_|_| |_\__, | / / / /
 =========|_|==============|___/=/_/_/_/
 :: Spring Boot ::        (v2.0.1.RELEASE)

2018-04-20 18:13:53.455  INFO 17292 --- [  restartedMain] c.p.cardatabase.CardatabaseApplication   : Starting CardatabaseApplication on HHMX4717 with PID 17292 (C:\Users\h01270
2018-04-20 18:13:53.457  INFO 17292 --- [  restartedMain] c.p.cardatabase.CardatabaseApplication   : No active profile set, falling back to default profiles: default
2018-04-20 18:13:53.546  INFO 17292 --- [  restartedMain] ConfigServletWebServerApplicationContext : Refreshing org.springframework.boot.web.servlet.context.AnnotationConfigSer
2018-04-20 18:13:55.207  INFO 17292 --- [  restartedMain] o.s.b.w.embedded.tomcat.TomcatWebServer  : Tomcat initialized with port(s): 8080 (http)
2018-04-20 18:13:55.231  INFO 17292 --- [  restartedMain] o.apache.catalina.core.StandardService   : Starting service [Tomcat]
2018-04-20 18:13:55.231  INFO 17292 --- [  restartedMain] org.apache.catalina.core.StandardEngine  : Starting Servlet Engine: Apache Tomcat/8.5.29
2018-04-20 18:13:55.239  INFO 17292 --- [ost-startStop-1] o.a.catalina.core.AprLifecycleListener   : The APR based Apache Tomcat Native library which allows optimal performance
2018-04-20 18:13:55.336  INFO 17292 --- [ost-startStop-1] o.a.c.c.C.[Tomcat].[localhost].[/]       : Initializing Spring embedded WebApplicationContext
2018-04-20 18:13:55.337  INFO 17292 --- [ost-startStop-1] o.s.web.context.ContextLoader            : Root WebApplicationContext: initialization completed in 1795 ms
2018-04-20 18:13:55.493  INFO 17292 --- [ost-startStop-1] o.s.b.w.servlet.ServletRegistrationBean  : Servlet dispatcherServlet mapped to [/]
2018-04-20 18:13:55.499  INFO 17292 --- [ost-startStop-1] o.s.b.w.servlet.FilterRegistrationBean   : Mapping filter: 'characterEncodingFilter' to: [/*]
2018-04-20 18:13:55.500  INFO 17292 --- [ost-startStop-1] o.s.b.w.servlet.FilterRegistrationBean   : Mapping filter: 'hiddenHttpMethodFilter' to: [/*]
2018-04-20 18:13:55.500  INFO 17292 --- [ost-startStop-1] o.s.b.w.servlet.FilterRegistrationBean   : Mapping filter: 'httpPutFormContentFilter' to: [/*]
2018-04-20 18:13:55.500  INFO 17292 --- [ost-startStop-1] o.s.b.w.servlet.FilterRegistrationBean   : Mapping filter: 'requestContextFilter' to: [/*]
2018-04-20 18:13:55.657  INFO 17292 --- [  restartedMain] o.s.w.s.handler.SimpleUrlHandlerMapping  : Mapped URL path [/**/favicon.ico] onto handler of type [class org.springfra
2018-04-20 18:13:55.909  INFO 17292 --- [  restartedMain] s.w.s.m.m.a.RequestMappingHandlerAdapter : Looking for @ControllerAdvice: org.springframework.boot.web.servlet.context
2018-04-20 18:13:55.997  INFO 17292 --- [  restartedMain] s.w.s.m.m.a.RequestMappingHandlerMapping : Mapped "{[/error]}" onto public org.springframework.http.ResponseEntity<jav
2018-04-20 18:13:55.998  INFO 17292 --- [  restartedMain] s.w.s.m.m.a.RequestMappingHandlerMapping : Mapped "{[/error],produces=[text/html]}" onto public org.springframework.we
2018-04-20 18:13:56.032  INFO 17292 --- [  restartedMain] o.s.w.s.handler.SimpleUrlHandlerMapping  : Mapped URL path [/webjars/**] onto handler of type [class org.springframewo
2018-04-20 18:13:56.032  INFO 17292 --- [  restartedMain] o.s.w.s.handler.SimpleUrlHandlerMapping  : Mapped URL path [/**] onto handler of type [class org.springframework.web.s
2018-04-20 18:13:56.213  INFO 17292 --- [  restartedMain] o.s.b.d.a.OptionalLiveReloadServer       : LiveReload server is running on port 35729
2018-04-20 18:13:56.245  INFO 17292 --- [  restartedMain] o.s.j.e.a.AnnotationMBeanExporter         : Registering beans for JMX exposure on startup
2018-04-20 18:13:56.361  INFO 17292 --- [  restartedMain] o.s.b.w.embedded.tomcat.TomcatWebServer  : Tomcat started on port(s): 8080 (http) with context path ''
2018-04-20 18:13:56.368  INFO 17292 --- [  restartedMain] c.p.cardatabase.CardatabaseApplication   : Started CardatabaseApplication in 3.315 seconds (JVM running for 4.345)
```

In the root of our project there is the `pom.xml` file, that is the Maven configuration file for
our project. If you look at the dependencies inside the file, you can see that there are now
dependencies that we selected on the Spring Initializr page. There is also a test dependency
included automatically without any selection. In the next chapters, we are going to add
more functionality to our application, and then we will add more dependencies manually
to the `pom.xml` file:

```xml
<dependencies>
  <dependency>
    <groupId>org.springframework.boot</groupId>
    <artifactId>spring-boot-starter-web</artifactId>
  </dependency>
  <dependency>
    <groupId>org.springframework.boot</groupId>
    <artifactId>spring-boot-devtools</artifactId>
    <scope>runtime</scope>
  </dependency>
  <dependency>
    <groupId>org.springframework.boot</groupId>
    <artifactId>spring-boot-starter-test</artifactId>
    <scope>test</scope>
  </dependency>
</dependencies>
```

Let's look at the Spring Boot main class more carefully. At the beginning of the class, there is the @SpringBootApplication annotation. It is actually a combination of multiple annotations, such as, the following:

Annotation	Description
@EnableAutoConfiguration	Enables Spring Boot automatic configuration. Spring Boot will automatically configure your project based on dependencies. For example, if you have the spring-boot-starter-web dependency, Spring Boot assumes that you are developing a web application and configures your application accordingly.
@ComponentScan	Enables the Spring Boot component scan to find all components from your application.
@Configure	Defines the class that can be used as a source of bean definitions.

The following code shows the Spring Boot application's main class:

```
import org.springframework.boot.SpringApplication;
import org.springframework.boot.autoconfigure.SpringBootApplication;

@SpringBootApplication
public class CardatabaseApplication {

  public static void main(String[] args) {
    SpringApplication.run(CardatabaseApplication.class, args);
  }
}
```

The execution of the application starts from the main method, as in standard Java applications.

> It is recommended to locate the main application class in the root package above other classes. Quite a common reason for an application to not work correctly is due to a situation where Spring Boot can't find some critical classes.

Spring Boot development tools

Spring Boot development tools make the application development process easier. Projects will include the developer tools if the following dependency is added to the Maven `pom.xml` file:

```
<dependency>
  <groupId>org.springframework.boot</groupId>
  <artifactId>spring-boot-devtools</artifactId>
  <scope>runtime</scope>
</dependency>
```

Development tools are disabled when you create a fully-packed production version of your application.

The application is automatically restarted when you make changes to your project classpath files. You can test that by adding one comment line to your `main` class. After saving the file, you can see in the console that the application has restarted:

```
package com.packt.cardatabase;

import org.springframework.boot.SpringApplication;
import org.springframework.boot.autoconfigure.SpringBootApplication;

@SpringBootApplication
public class CardatabaseApplication {

  public static void main(String[] args) {
    // After adding this comment the application is restarted
    SpringApplication.run(CardatabaseApplication.class, args);
  }
}
```

Logs and problem solving

Spring Boot starter packages provide a logback, that we can use for logging without any configuration. The following sample code shows how to use logging:

```
import org.slf4j.Logger;
import org.slf4j.LoggerFactory;
import org.springframework.boot.SpringApplication;
import org.springframework.boot.autoconfigure.SpringBootApplication;

@SpringBootApplication
public class CardatabaseApplication {
```

```
   private static final Logger logger =
LoggerFactory.getLogger(CardatabaseApplication.class);
   public static void main(String[] args) {
      SpringApplication.run(CardatabaseApplication.class, args);
      logger.info("Hello Spring Boot");
   }
}
```

Logging messages can be seen in the console after you run the project:

There are seven different levels for logging—TRACE, DEBUG, INFO, WARN, ERROR, FATAL, and OFF. You can configure the level of logging in your Spring Boot application.properties file. The file can be found in the resources folder inside your project:

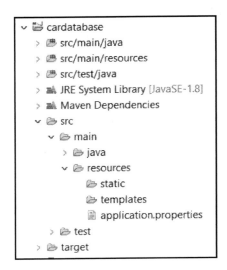

If we set the logging level to INFO, we can see log messages from levels that are under INFO (INFO, WARN, ERROR, and FATAL). In the following example, we set the log level for the root, but you can also set it at the package level:

```
logging.level.root=INFO
```

Now, when you run the project, you can't see the TRACE and DEBUG messages anymore. That might be a good setting for a production version of your application:

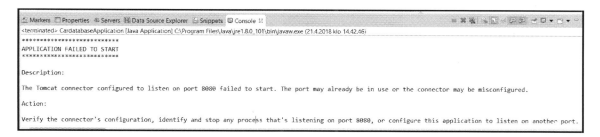

Spring Boot is using Apache Tomcat (http://tomcat.apache.org/) as an application server, by default. As a default, Tomcat is running in port 8080. You can change the port in the application.properties file. The following setting will start Tomcat in port 8081:

```
server.port=8081
```

If the port is occupied, the application won't start and you will see the following message in the console:

```
***************************
APPLICATION FAILED TO START
***************************

Description:

The Tomcat connector configured to listen on port 8080 failed to start. The port may already be in use or the connector may be misconfigured.

Action:

Verify the connector's configuration, identify and stop any process that's listening on port 8080, or configure this application to listen on another port.
```

You have to stop the process that is listening on port 8080 or use another port in your Spring Boot application.

Installing MariaDB

In the next chapter, we are going to use MariaDB, and therefore we will install it locally to your computer. MariaDB is a widely used open source relational database. MariaDB is available for Windows and Linux, and you can download the latest stable version from https://downloads.mariadb.org/. MariaDB is developed under a GNU GPL 2 license.

For Windows, there is the MSI installer, that we will use here. Download the installer and execute it. Install all features from the installation wizard:

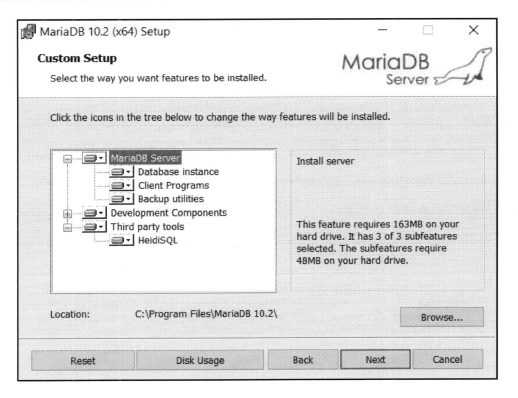

In the next step, you should give the password for the root user. This password is needed in the next chapter, when we connect to the database with our application:

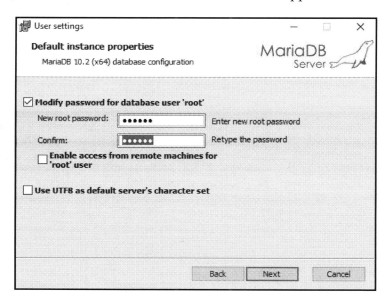

In the next phase, we can use the default settings:

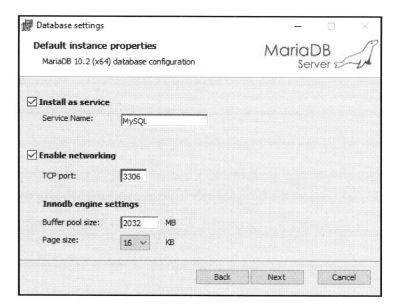

Now the installation starts, and MariaDB will be installed to your local computer. The installation wizard will install **HeidiSQL** for us. This is a graphically easy-to-use database client. We will use this to add a new database and make queries to our database. You can also use the Command Prompt included in the installation package:

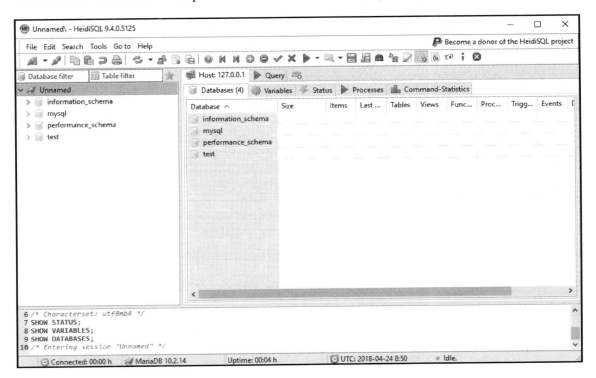

Summary

In this chapter, we installed the tools that are needed for backend development with Spring Boot. For Java development, we used Eclipse IDE, that is a widely used programming IDE. We created a new Spring Boot project by using the Spring Initializr page. After creating the project, it was imported to Eclipse and, finally, executed. We also covered how to solve common problems with Spring Boot and how to find important error and log messages. Finally, we installed a MariaDB database, that we are going to use in the next chapter.

Questions

1. What is Spring Boot?
2. What is Eclipse IDE?
3. What is Maven?
4. How do we create a Spring Boot project?
5. How do we run a Spring Boot project?
6. How do we use logging with Spring Boot?
7. How do we find error and log messages in Eclipse?

Further reading

Packt has other great resources for learning about Spring Boot:

- https://www.packtpub.com/application-development/learning-spring-boot-20-second-edition
- https://www.packtpub.com/web-development/spring-boot-getting-started-integrated-course

2
Using JPA to Create and Access a Database

This chapter covers how to use JPA with Spring Boot. We will create a database by using entity classes. In the first phase, we will be using the H2 in-memory database for development and demonstration purposes. H2 is an in-memory SQL database that is really good for fast development or demonstration purposes. In the second phase, we will move from H2 to use MariaDB. This chapter also describes the creation of CRUD repositories and a one-to-many connection between database tables.

In this chapter, we will look at the following:

- Basics and benefits of using JPA
- How to define a database by using entity classes
- How to create Spring Boot backend with a database

Technical requirements

Java SDK version 8 or higher is necessary for the usage of Spring Boot (`http://www.oracle.com/technetwork/java/javase/downloads/index.html`).

A MariaDB installation is necessary for the creation of the database application (`https://downloads.mariadb.org/`).

Basics of ORM, JPA, and Hibernate

Object-Relational Mapping (ORM) is a technique that allows you to fetch and manipulate from a database by using an object-oriented programming paradigm. ORM is really nice for programmers because it relies on object-oriented concepts, not on database structure. It also makes development much faster and reduces the amount of source code. ORM is mostly independent of the databases and developers don't have to worry about vendor-specific SQL statements.

Java Persistent API (JPA) provides object-relational mapping for Java developers. The JPA entity is a Java class that presents the structure of a database table. The fields of an entity class present the columns of the database tables.

Hibernate is the most popular Java-based JPA implementation, and it is used in Spring Boot as a default. Hibernate is a mature product and it is widely used in large-scale applications.

Creating the entity classes

An entity class is a simple Java class that is annotated with JPA's `@Entity` annotation. Entity classes use the standard JavaBean naming convention and have proper getter and setter methods. The class fields have private visibility.

JPA creates a database table called the name of the class when the application is initialized. If you want to use some other name for the database table, you can use the `@Table` annotation.

To be able to use JPA and the H2 database, we have to add the following dependencies to the `pom.xml` file:

```
<dependency>
  <groupId>org.springframework.boot</groupId>
  <artifactId>spring-boot-starter-data-jpa</artifactId>
</dependency>
<dependency>
    <groupId>com.h2database</groupId>
    <artifactId>h2</artifactId>
    <scope>runtime</scope>
</dependency>
```

Following are the steps for creating entity classes:

1. To create an entity class in Spring Boot, we will first create our own package for entities. The package should be created under the root package.
2. Activate the root package in Eclipse **Project Explorer** and right-click to show a menu.
3. From the menu, select **New | Package**. The following screenshot shows the creation of package for entity classes:

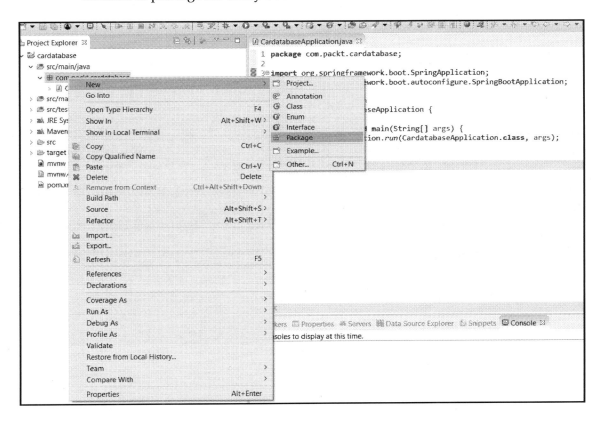

4. We name our package `com.packt.cardatabase.domain`:

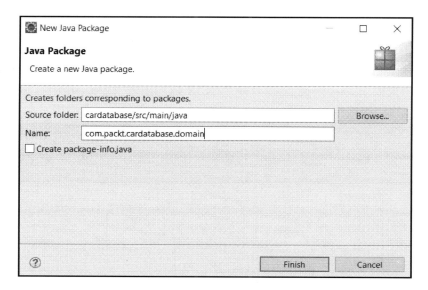

5. Next, we create our entity class. Activate a new entity package, right-click, and select **New** | **Class** from the menu. Because we are going to create a car database, the name of the entity class is `Car`. Type `Car` in the **Name** field and then press the **Finish** button:

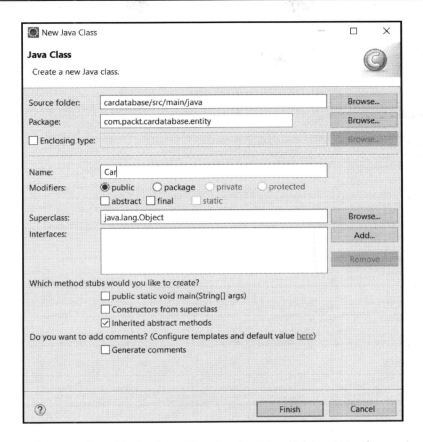

6. Open the `Car` class file in the editor by double-clicking it in the project explorer. First, we have to annotate the class with the `@Entity` annotation. The `Entity` annotation is imported from the `javax.persistence` package:

```
package com.packt.cardatabase.domain;

import javax.persistence.Entity;

@Entity
public class Car {

}
```

You can use the *Ctrl + Shift + O* shortcut in Eclipse IDE to import missing packages automatically.

7. Next, we add some fields to our class. The entity class fields are mapped to database table columns. The entity class must also contain a unique ID that is used as a primary key in the database:

```
package com.packt.cardatabase.domain;

import javax.persistence.Entity;
import javax.persistence.GeneratedValue;
import javax.persistence.GenerationType;
import javax.persistence.Id;

@Entity
public class Car {
  @Id
  @GeneratedValue(strategy=GenerationType.AUTO)
  private long id;
  private String brand, model, color, registerNumber;
  private int year, price;
}
```

The primary key is defined by using the @Id annotation. The @GeneratedValue annotation defines that the ID is automatically generated by the database. We can also define our key generation strategy. Type AUTO means that the JPA provider selects the best strategy for a particular database. You can also create a composite primary key by annotating multiple attributes with the @Id annotation.

The database columns are named according to class field naming by default. If you want to use some other naming convention, you can use the @Column annotation. With the @Column annotation, you can also define the column's length and whether the column is nullable. The following code shows an example of using the @Column annotation. With this definition, the column's name in the database is desc and the length of the column is 512 and it is not nullable:

```
@Column(name="desc", nullable=false, length=512)
private String description
```

8. Finally we add getters, setters and constructors with attributes to the entity class. We don't need an ID field in our constructor due to automatic ID generation. The source code of `Car` entity class constructors follows:

> Eclipse provides the automatic addition of getters, setters and constructors. Activate your cursor inside the class and right-click. From the menu, select **Source | Generate Getters and Setters...** or **Source | Generate Constructor using fields...**

```java
package com.packt.cardatabase.domain;

import javax.persistence.Entity;
import javax.persistence.GeneratedValue;
import javax.persistence.GenerationType;
import javax.persistence.Id;

@Entity
public class Car {
  @Id
  @GeneratedValue(strategy=GenerationType.AUTO)
  private long id;
  private String brand, model, color, registerNumber;
  private int year, price;
  public Car() {}
  public Car(String brand, String model, String color,
    String registerNumber, int year, int price) {
    super();
    this.brand = brand;
    this.model = model;
    this.color = color;
    this.registerNumber = registerNumber;
    this.year = year;
    this.price = price;
  }
```

The following is the source code of `Car` entity class getters and setters:

```java
public String getBrand() {
  return brand;
}
public void setBrand(String brand) {
  this.brand = brand;
}
public String getModel() {
  return model;
}
```

```java
public void setModel(String model) {
  this.model = model;
}
public String getColor() {
  return color;
}
public void setColor(String color) {
  this.color = color;
}
public String getRegisterNumber() {
  return registerNumber;
}
public void setRegisterNumber(String registerNumber) {
  this.registerNumber = registerNumber;
}
public int getYear() {
  return year;
}
public void setYear(int year) {
  this.year = year;
}
public int getPrice() {
  return price;
}
public void setPrice(int price) {
  this.price = price;
}
}
```

The table called `car` must be created in the database when we run the application. To ensure that, we will add one new property to the `application.properties` file. This enables the logging of SQL statements to the console:

```
spring.jpa.show-sql=true
```

We can now see the table creation statements when running the application:

H2 provides a web-based console that can be used to explore a database and execute SQL statements. To enable the console, we have to add the following lines to the `application.properties` file. The first setting enables the H2 console and the second setting defines the endpoint that we can use to access the console:

```
spring.h2.console.enabled=true
spring.h2.console.path=/h2-console
```

You can access the H2 console by navigating to `localhost:8080/h2-console` with the web browser. Use `jdbc:h2:mem:testdb` as the **JDBC URL** and leave the **Password** field empty in the login window. Press the **Connect** button to log in to the console:

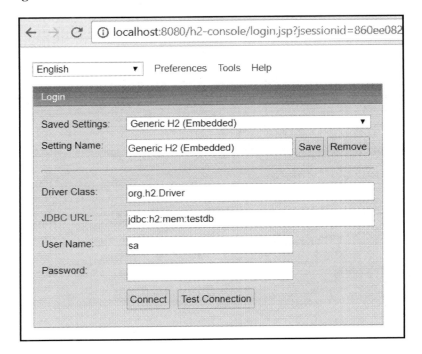

Now you can see our `car` table in the database. You may notice that the register number has an underscore between the words. That is due to the camel case naming of the attribute (`registerNumber`):

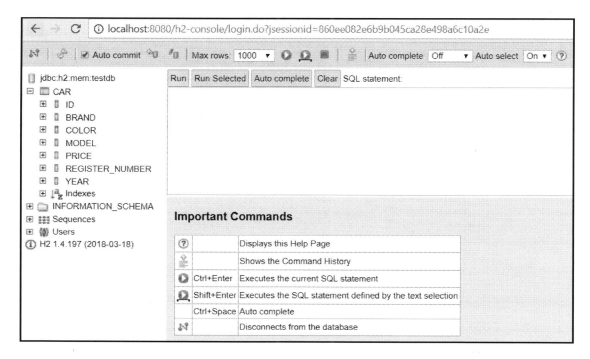

Creating CRUD repositories

The Spring Boot Data JPA provides a `CrudRepository` interface for CRUD operations. It provides CRUD functionalities to our entity class.

We will now create our repository in the domain package, as follows:

1. Create a new class called CarRepository in the domain package and modify the file according to the following code snippet:

```
package com.packt.cardatabase.domain;

import org.springframework.data.repository.CrudRepository;

public interface CarRepository extends CrudRepository <Car, Long> {

}
```

Our CarRepository now extends the Spring Boot JPA CrudRepository interface. <Car, Long> type arguments define that this is the repository for the Car entity class and the type of the ID field is long.

CrudRepository provides multiple CRUD methods that we can now start to use. The following table lists the most commonly used methods:

Method	Description
long count()	Returns the number of entities
Iterable<T> findAll()	Returns all items of given type
Optional<T> findById(ID Id)	Returns one item by id
void delete(T entity)	Deletes an entity
void deleteAll()	Deletes all entities of the repository
<S extends T> save(S entity)	Saves an entity

If the method returns only one item, the Optional<T> is returned instead of T. The Optional class gets introduced in Java 8 SE. Optional is a type of single value container that either has value or doesn't. By using Optional, we can prevent null pointer exceptions.

2. Now we are ready to add some demonstration data to our H2 database. For that, we will use the Spring Boot CommandLineRunner. The CommandLineRunner interface allows us to execute additional code before the application has fully started. Therefore, it is a good point to add demo data to your database. CommandLineRunner is located inside the main class:

```
import org.springframework.boot.CommandLineRunner;
import org.springframework.boot.SpringApplication;
import org.springframework.boot.autoconfigure.SpringBootApplication;
import org.springframework.context.annotation.Bean;
```

```
@SpringBootApplication
public class CardatabaseApplication {

  public static void main(String[] args) {
    SpringApplication.run(CardatabaseApplication.class, args);
  }
  @Bean
  CommandLineRunner runner(){
    return args -> {
      // Place your code here
    };
  }
}
```

3. Next, we have to inject our car repository into the main class into be able to save new car objects to the database. An `@Autowired` annotation is used to enable dependency injection. The dependency injection allows us to pass dependencies into a object. After we have injected the repository class, we can use the CRUD methods it provides. The following sample code shows how to insert a few cars to the database:

```
import org.springframework.beans.factory.annotation.Autowired;
import org.springframework.boot.CommandLineRunner;
import org.springframework.boot.SpringApplication;
import org.springframework.boot.autoconfigure.SpringBootApplication;
import org.springframework.context.annotation.Bean;

import com.packt.cardatabase.domain.Car;
import com.packt.cardatabase.domain.CarRepository;

@SpringBootApplication
public class CardatabaseApplication {
  @Autowired
  private CarRepository repository;
  public static void main(String[] args) {
    SpringApplication.run(CardatabaseApplication.class, args);
  }
  @Bean
  CommandLineRunner runner(){
    return args -> {
      // Save demo data to database
      repository.save(new Car("Ford", "Mustang", "Red",
        "ADF-1121", 2017, 59000));
      repository.save(new Car("Nissan", "Leaf", "White",
        "SSJ-3002", 2014, 29000));
```

```
        repository.save(new Car("Toyota", "Prius", "Silver",
          "KKO-0212", 2018, 39000));
    };
  }
}
```

`Insert` statements can be seen in the Eclipse console after the application has been executed:

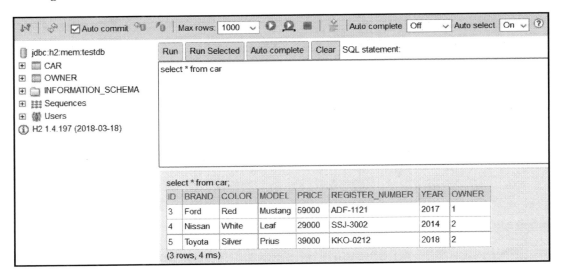

You can also use the H2 console to fetch cars from the database, as seen in the following screenshot:

ID	BRAND	COLOR	MODEL	PRICE	REGISTER_NUMBER	YEAR	OWNER
3	Ford	Red	Mustang	59000	ADF-1121	2017	1
4	Nissan	White	Leaf	29000	SSJ-3002	2014	2
5	Toyota	Silver	Prius	39000	KKO-0212	2018	2

(3 rows, 4 ms)

You can define your own queries in the Spring Data repositories. The query must start with a prefix, for example, findBy. After the prefix, you define the entity class fields that are used in the query. The following is a sample code of three simple queries:

```
import java.util.List;

import org.springframework.data.repository.CrudRepository;

public interface CarRepository extends CrudRepository <Car, Long> {
  // Fetch cars by brand
  List<Car> findByBrand(String brand);

  // Fetch cars by color
  List<Car> findByColor(String color);

  // Fetch cars by year
  List<Car> findByYear(int year);

}
```

There can be multiple fields after the By keyword, concatenated with the And or Or keywords:

```
package com.packt.cardatabase.domain;

import java.util.List;

import org.springframework.data.repository.CrudRepository;

public interface CarRepository extends CrudRepository <Car, Long> {
  // Fetch cars by brand and model
  List<Car> findByBrandAndModel(String brand, String model);

  // Fetch cars by brand or color
  List<Car> findByBrandOrColor(String brand, String color);
}
```

Queries can be sorted by using the OrderBy keyword in the query method:

```
package com.packt.cardatabase.domain;

import java.util.List;

import org.springframework.data.repository.CrudRepository;

public interface CarRepository extends CrudRepository <Car, Long> {
  // Fetch cars by brand and sort by year
```

```
    List<Car> findByBrandOrderByYearAsc(String brand);
}
```

You can also create queries by using SQL statements, via the @Query annotation. The following example shows the usage of a SQL query in CrudRepository:

```
package com.packt.cardatabase.domain;

import java.util.List;

import org.springframework.data.repository.CrudRepository;

public interface CarRepository extends CrudRepository <Car, Long> {
    // Fetch cars by brand using SQL
    @Query("select c from Car c where c.brand = ?1")
    List<Car> findByBrand(String brand);
}
```

You can use also more advanced expressions with the @Query annotation, for example, like. The following example shows the usage of the like query in CrudRepository:

```
package com.packt.cardatabase.domain;

import java.util.List;

import org.springframework.data.repository.CrudRepository;

public interface CarRepository extends CrudRepository <Car, Long> {
    // Fetch cars by brand using SQL
    @Query("select c from Car c where c.brand like %?1")
    List<Car> findByBrandEndsWith(String brand);
}
```

Spring Data JPA also provides PagingAndSortingRepository, which extends CrudRepository. It offers methods for fetching entities using pagination and sorting. This is a good option if you are dealing with larger amounts of data. PagingAndSortingRepository can be created similarly to what we did with CrudRepository:

```
package com.packt.cardatabase.domain;

import org.springframework.data.repository.PagingAndSortingRepository;
```

```
public interface CarRepository extends PagingAndSortingRepository<Car,
Long> {

}
```

In this case, you now have the two new additional methods that the repository provides:

Method	Description
Iterable<T> findAll(Sort sort)	Returns all entities sorted by the given options
Page<T> findAll(Pageable pageable)	Returns all entities according to given paging options

Relationships between tables

Next, we create a new table called `owner` that has a one-to-many relationship with the `car` table. The owner can own multiple cars, but a car can have only one owner. The following UML diagram shows the relationship between the tables:

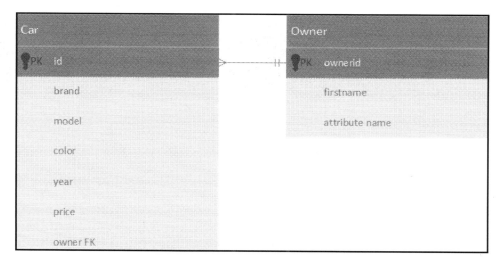

The following are the steps for creating a new table:

1. First, we create the `Owner` entity and repository in the `domain` package. The `Owner` entity and repository are created similarly to what we did with the `Car` class. The following is the source code of the `Owner` entity class and `OwnerRepository`:

   ```
   // Owner.java
   ```

```
package com.packt.cardatabase.domain;

import javax.persistence.Entity;
import javax.persistence.GeneratedValue;
import javax.persistence.GenerationType;
import javax.persistence.Id;

@Entity
public class Owner {
  @Id
  @GeneratedValue(strategy=GenerationType.AUTO)
  private long ownerid;
  private String firstname, lastname;
  public Owner() {}
  public Owner(String firstname, String lastname) {
    super();
    this.firstname = firstname;
    this.lastname = lastname;
  }

  public long getOwnerid() {
    return ownerid;
  }
  public void setOwnerid(long ownerid) {
    this.ownerid = ownerid;
  }
  public String getFirstname() {
    return firstname;
  }
  public void setFirstname(String firstname) {
    this.firstname = firstname;
  }
  public String getLastname() {
    return lastname;
  }
  public void setLastname(String lastname) {
    this.lastname = lastname;
  }
}

// OwnerRepository.java

package com.packt.cardatabase.domain;

import org.springframework.data.repository.CrudRepository;
```

```
public interface OwnerRepository extends CrudRepository<Owner, Long>
{

}
```

2. In this phase, it is good to check that everything is done correctly. Run the project and check that both database tables are created and that there are no errors in the console. The following screenshot shows the console messages when tables are created:

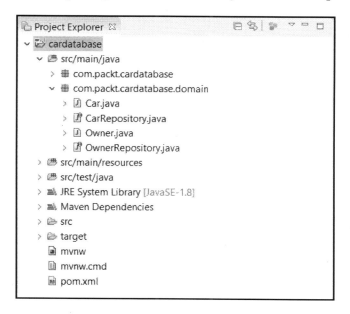

Now, our domain package contains two entity classes and repositories:

3. The one-to-many relationship can be added by using the @ManyToOne and @OneToMany annotations. In the car entity class, which contains a foreign key, you will define the relationship with the @ManyToOne annotation. Also, add the getter and setter for the owner field. It is recommended using FetchType.LAZY for all associations. For toMany relationships, that is the default value, but for toOne relationships, you should define it. FetchType defines the strategy for fetching data from the database. The value can be either EAGER or LAZY. In our case, the lazy strategy means that when the owner is fetched from the database, all the cars associated with the owner will be fetched when needed. Eager means that the cars will be fetched immediately with the owner. The following source code shows how to define a one-to-many relationship in the Car class:

```
// Car.java

@ManyToOne(fetch = FetchType.LAZY)
@JoinColumn(name = "owner")
private Owner owner;

//Getter and setter
public Owner getOwner() {
  return owner;
}

public void setOwner(Owner owner) {
  this.owner = owner;
}
```

In the owner entity site, the relationship is defined with the @OneToMany annotation. The type of the field is List<Car> because the owner may have multiple cars. Add also the getter and setter for that:

```
// Owner.java

@OneToMany(cascade = CascadeType.ALL, mappedBy="owner")
private List<Car> cars;

//Getter and setter
public List<Car> getCars() {
  return cars;
}
public void setCars(List<Car> cars) {
  this.cars = cars;
}
```

The @OneToMany annotation has two attributes that we are using. The cascade attribute defines how cascading affects the entities. The attribute setting ALL means that if the owner is deleted, the cars linked to that owner are deleted as well. The mappedBy="owner" attribute setting tells us that the Car class has the owner field, which is the foreign key for this relationship.

When you run the project, you can see from the console that the relationship is now created:

4. Now, we can add some owners to the database with CommandLineRunner. Let's also modify the Car entity classes constructor and add an owner there:

```java
// Car.java constructor

public Car(String brand, String model, String color,
String registerNumber, int year, int price, Owner owner) {
    super();
    this.brand = brand;
    this.model = model;
    this.color = color;
    this.registerNumber = registerNumber;
    this.year = year;
    this.price = price;
    this.owner = owner;
}
```

5. We first create two owner objects and save these to the database. For saving the owners, we also have to inject the `OwnerRepository` into the main class. Then we connect the owners to the cars by using the `Car` constructor. The following is the source code of the application main class `CardatabaseApplication`:

```
@SpringBootApplication
public class CardatabaseApplication {
  // Inject repositories
  @Autowired
  private CarRepository repository;

  @Autowired
  private OwnerRepository orepository;
  public static void main(String[] args) {
    SpringApplication.run(CardatabaseApplication.class, args);
  }
  @Bean
  CommandLineRunner runner() {
    return args -> {
      // Add owner objects and save these to db
      Owner owner1 = new Owner("John" , "Johnson");
      Owner owner2 = new Owner("Mary" , "Robinson");
      orepository.save(owner1);
      orepository.save(owner2);
      // Add car object with link to owners and save these to db.
      Car car = new Car("Ford", "Mustang", "Red",
          "ADF-1121", 2017, 59000, owner1);
      repository.save(car);
      car = new Car("Nissan", "Leaf", "White",
          "SSJ-3002", 2014, 29000, owner2);
      repository.save(car);
      car = new Car("Toyota", "Prius", "Silver",
          "KKO-0212", 2018, 39000, owner2);
      repository.save(car);
    };
  }
}
```

If you now run the application and fetch cars from the database, you can see that the owners are now linked to the cars:

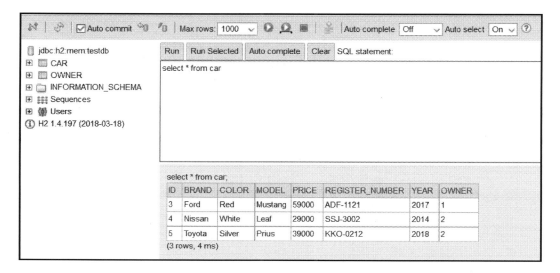

If you want to create many-to-many relationship instead, which means, in practice, that an owner can have multiple cars and a car can have multiple owners, you should use the @ManyToMany annotation. In our example application, we will use a one-to-many relationship, but there follows an example of how to change the relationship to many-to-many. In a many-to-many relationship, it is recommended using Set instead of List with hibernate:

1. In the Car entity class many-to-many relationship, define the getters and setters in the following way:

```
@ManyToMany(mappedBy = "cars")
private Set<Owner> owners;

public Set<Owner> getOwners() {
  return owners;
}

public void setOwners(Set<Owner> owners) {
  this.owners = owners;
}
```

In the owner entity, the definition as follows:

```
@ManyToMany(cascade = CascadeType.MERGE)
@JoinTable(name = "car_owner", joinColumns = { @JoinColumn(name =
  "ownerid") }, inverseJoinColumns = { @JoinColumn(name = "id") })
private Set<Car> cars = new HashSet<Car>(0);

public Set<Car> getCars() {
  return cars;
}

public void setCars(Set<Car> cars) {
  this.cars = cars;
}
```

2. Now, if you run the application, there will be a new join table that is created between the `car` and `owner` tables. The join table is defined by using the `@JoinTable` annotation. With the annotation, we can set the name of the join table and join columns. The following is a screenshot of the database structure when using a many-to-many relationship:

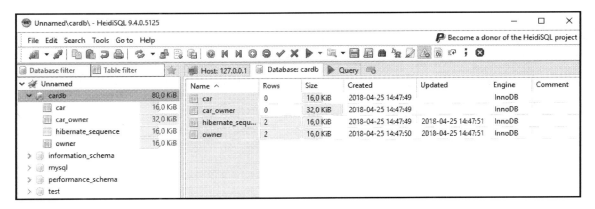

Setting up the MariaDB database

Now, we switch our database from H2 to MariaDB. The database tables are still created automatically by JPA. But before we run our application, we have to create a database for it. The database can be created by using HeidiSQL. Open HeidiSQL, and follow these steps:

1. Right-click your mouse inside the database list.
2. Then, select **New** | **Database**:

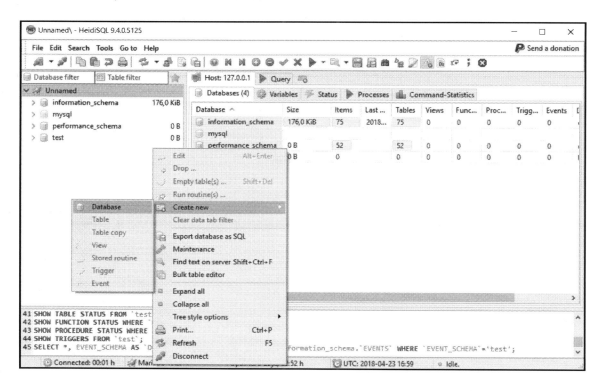

3. Let's name our database `cardb`. After you press **OK**, you should see the new `cardb` in the database list:

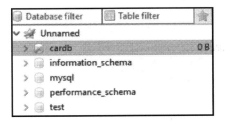

4. In the application, we add a MariaDB dependency to the `pom.xml` file and remove the H2 dependency that we don't need any more:

```
<dependency>
   <groupId>org.mariadb.jdbc</groupId>
   <artifactId>mariadb-java-client</artifactId>
</dependency>
```

5. In the `application.properties` file, you define the database connection. First, you will define the database's `url`, `username`, `password` and database driver class. The `spring.jpa.generate-ddl` setting defines whether JPA should initialize the database (`true`/`false`). The `spring.jpa.hibernate.ddl-auto` setting defines the behavior of the database initialization. The possible values are `none`, `validate`, `update`, `create`, and `create-drop`. Create-drop means that the database is created when an application starts and it is dropped when the application is stopped. Create-drop is also a default value if you don't define any. Create value only creates the database when the application is started. Update value creates the database and updates the schema if it is changed:

```
spring.datasource.url=jdbc:mariadb://localhost:3306/cardb
spring.datasource.username=root
spring.datasource.password=YOUR_PASSWORD
spring.datasource.driver-class-name=org.mariadb.jdbc.Driver

spring.jpa.generate-ddl=true
spring.jpa.hibernate.ddl-auto=create-drop
```

6. Now, after running the application, you should see the tables in MariaDB. The following screenshot shows the HeidiSQL UI after the database has been created. Your application is now ready to be used with MariaDB:

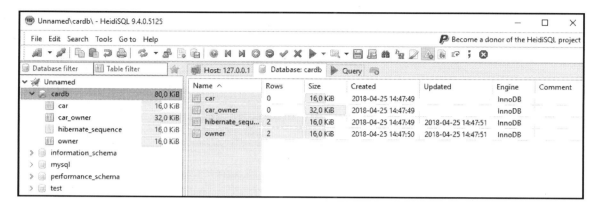

Summary

In this chapter, we used JPA to create our Spring Boot application database. First, we created entity classes, which are mapped to database tables. Then, we created `CrudRepository` for our entity class and that provides CRUD operations for the entity. After that, we managed to add some demo data to our database by using `CommandLineRunner`. We also created one-to-many relations between two entities. At the beginning of the chapter, we used the H2 in-memory database, while at the end, we switched the database to MariaDB. In the next chapter we will create RESTful web service to our backend.

Questions

1. What are ORM, JPA, and Hibernate?
2. How can you create an entity class?
3. How can you create `CrudRepository`?
4. How does the `CrudRepository` provide for your application?
5. How can you create a one-to-many relationship between tables?
6. How can you add demo data to a database with Spring Boot?
7. How can you access the H2 console?
8. How can you connect your Spring Boot application to MariaDB?

Further reading

Packt has other great resources for learning Spring Boot:

- https://www.packtpub.com/application-development/learning-spring-boot-20-second-edition
- https://www.packtpub.com/web-development/spring-boot-getting-started-integrated-course

Creating a RESTful Web Service with Spring Boot

3

In this chapter, we will first create a RESTful web service using the controller class. After that, we will demonstrate how to use Spring Data REST to create a RESTful web service that also covers all CRUD functionalities automatically. We are using the database application that we created in the previous chapter as a starting point.

In this chapter, we will look into the following:

- What the RESTful web service is
- How to create a RESTful web service with Spring Boot
- How to test the RESTful web service

Technical requirements

The Spring Boot application that has been created in previous chapters is necessary.

Postman, cURL, or another suitable tool for transferring data using various HTTP methods is necessary.

Creating a RESTful web service with Spring Boot

Web services are applications that communicate over the internet using the HTTP protocol. There are many different types of web service architectures, but the main idea across all designs is the same. In this book, we are creating a RESTful web service from what is a really popular design nowadays.

Basics of REST

REST (Representational State Transfer) is an architectural style for creating web services. REST is not standard, but it defines a set of constraints defined by Roy Fielding. The six constraints are the following:

- **Stateless**: The server doesn't hold any information about the client state.
- **Client server**: The client and server act independently. The server does not send any information without a request from the client.
- **Cacheable**: Many clients often request the same resources, therefore it is useful to cache responses in order to improve performance.
- **Uniform interface**: Requests from different clients look the same. Clients may be, for example, a browser, a Java application, and a mobile application.
- **Layered system**: REST allows us to use a layered system architecture.
- **Code on demand**: This is an optional constraint.

The uniform interface is an important constraint and it defines that every REST architecture should have following elements:

- **Identification of resources**: There are resources with their unique identifiers, for example, URIs in web-based REST services. REST resources should expose easily understood directory structure URIs. Therefore, a good resource naming strategy is very important.
- **Resource manipulation through representation**: When making a request to a resource, the server responds with a representation of the resource. Typically, the format of the representation is JSON or XML.
- **Self descriptive messages**: Messages should have enough information that the server knows how to process them.
- **Hypermedia and the Engine of Application State (HATEOAS)**: Responses can contain links to other areas of service.

The RESTful web service that we are going to develop in the following topics follows the REST architectural principles.

Creating a RESTful web service

In Spring Boot, all the HTTP requests are handled by controller classes. To be able to create a RESTful web service, first, we have to create a controller class. We will create our own Java package for our controller:

1. Activate the root package in the Eclipse **Project Explorer** and right-click. Select **New | Package** from the menu. We will name our new package com.packt.cardatabase.web:

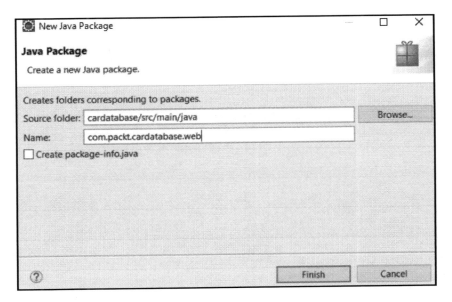

2. Next, we will create a new controller class in a new web package. Activate the `com.packt.cardatabase.web` package in the Eclipse project explorer and right-click. Select **New | Class** from the menu. We will name our class `CarController`:

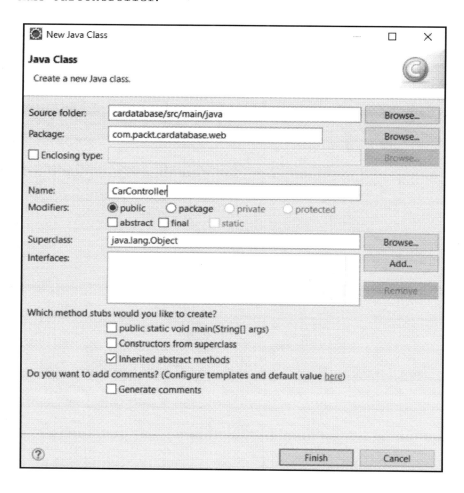

3. Now, your project structure should look like the following screenshot:

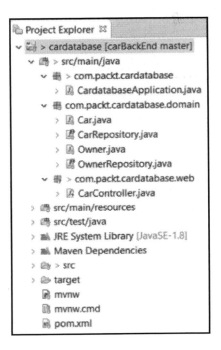

If you create classes in a wrong package accidentally, you can drag and drop the files between packages in the Eclipse **Project Explorer**. Sometimes, the Eclipse **Project Explorer** view might not be rendered correctly when you make some changes. Refreshing the project explorer helps (Activate **Project Explorer** and press *F5*).

4. Open your controller class in the editor window and add the @RestController annotation before the class definition. See the following source code. The @RestController annotation identifies that this class will be the controller for the RESTful web service:

```
package com.packt.cardatabase.web;

import org.springframework.web.bind.annotation.RestController;

@RestController
public class CarController {
}
```

5. Next, we add a new method inside our controller class. The method is annotated with the @RequestMapping annotation, which defines the endpoint that the method is mapped to. Following, you can see the sample source code. In this example, when a user navigates to the /cars endpoint, the getCars() method is executed:

```
package com.packt.cardatabase.web;

import org.springframework.web.bind.annotation.RestController;

@RestController
public class CarController {
  @RequestMapping("/cars")
  public Iterable<Car> getCars() {
  }
}
```

The getCars() method returns all the car objects, which are then marshalled to JSON objects by Jackson library.

 By default, @RequestMapping handles all the HTTP method (GET, PUT, POST, and more) requests. You can define which method is accepted with the following @RequestMapping("/cars", method=GET) parameter. Now, this method handles only GET requests from the /cars endpoint.

6. To be able to return cars from the database, we have to inject our `CarRepository` into the controller. Then, we can use the `findAll()` method that the repository provides to fetch all cars. The following source code shows the controller code:

```
package com.packt.cardatabase.web;

import org.springframework.beans.factory.annotation.Autowired;
import org.springframework.web.bind.annotation.RequestMapping;
import org.springframework.web.bind.annotation.RestController;

import com.packt.cardatabase.domain.Car;
import com.packt.cardatabase.domain.CarRepository;

@RestController
public class CarController {
  @Autowired
  private CarRepository repository;
  @RequestMapping("/cars")
  public Iterable<Car> getCars() {
    return repository.findAll();
  }
}
```

7. Now, we are ready to run our application and navigate to `localhost:8080/cars`. We can see that there is something wrong, and the application seems to be in an infinite loop. That happens due to our one-to-many relationship between the car and owner tables. So, what happens in practice—first, the car is serialized, and it contains an owner that is then serialized, and that, in turn, contains cars that are then serialized... and so on. To avoid this, we have to add the `@JsonIgnore` annotation to the `cars` field in the `Owner` class:

```
// Owner.java

@OneToMany(cascade = CascadeType.ALL, mappedBy="owner")
@JsonIgnore
private List<Car> cars;
```

8. Now, when you run the application and navigate to `localhost:8080/cars`, everything should go as expected and you will get all the cars from the database in JSON format, as shown in the following screenshot:

```
[ ▼ 3 items, 502 bytes
  { ▼ 7 properties, 164 bytes
    "brand": "Ford",
    "model": "Mustang",
    "color": "Red",
    "registerNumber": "ADF-1121",
    "year": 2017,
    "price": 59000,
    "owner": { ▼ 3 properties, 53 bytes
      "ownerid": 1,
      "firstname": "John",
      "lastname": "Johnson"
    }
  },
  { ▼ 7 properties, 166 bytes
    "brand": "Nissan",
    "model": "Leaf",
    "color": "White",
    "registerNumber": "SSJ-3002",
    "year": 2014,
    "price": 29000,
    "owner": { ▼ 3 properties, 54 bytes
      "ownerid": 2,
      "firstname": "Mary",
      "lastname": "Robinson"
    }
  },
  { ▼ 7 properties, 166 bytes
    "brand": "Toyota",
    "model": "Prius",
    "color": "Silver",
    "registerNumber": "KKO-0212",
    "year": 2018,
    "price": 39000,
    "owner": { ▼ 3 properties, 54 bytes
      "ownerid": 2,
      "firstname": "Mary",
      "lastname": "Robinson"
    }
```

We have done our first RESTful web service, which return all the cars. Spring Boot provides a much more powerful way of creating RESTful Web Services and this is investigated in the next topic.

Using Spring Data REST

Spring Data REST is part of the Spring Data project. It offers an easy and fast way to implement RESTful Web Services with Spring. To start, using Spring Data REST you have to add the following dependency to the `pom.xml` file:

```xml
<dependency>
    <groupId>org.springframework.boot</groupId>
    <artifactId>spring-boot-starter-data-rest</artifactId>
</dependency>
```

By default, Spring Data REST finds all public repositories from the application and creates automatically RESTful Web Services for your entities.

You can define the endpoint of service in your `application.properties` file:

```
spring.data.rest.basePath=/api
```

Now you can access the RESTful web service from the `localhost:8080/api` endpoint. By calling the root endpoint of the service it returns the resources that are available. Spring Data REST returns JSON data in the **HAL (Hypertext Application Language)** format. The HAL format provides a set of conventions for expressing hyperlinks in JSON and it makes your RESTful web service easier to use for frontend developers:

We can see that there are links to the car and owner entity services. The Spring Data Rest service pathname is derived from the entity name. The name will then be pluralized and uncapitalized. For example, the entity Car service pathname will be named `cars`. The profile link is generated by Spring Data Rest and it contains application-specific metadata.

Now, we start to examine different services more carefully. There are multiple tools available for testing and consuming RESTful Web Services. In this book, we are using Postman, but you can use tools that you are familiar with, such as cURL. Postman can be acquired as a desktop application or as a browser plugin. cURL is also available for Windows 10 by using Windows Ubuntu Bash.

If you make a request to the cars endpoint http://localhost:8080/api/cars using the GET method, you will get a list of all the cars, as shown in the following screenshot:

In the JSON response, you can see that there is an array of cars and each car contains car specific data. All the cars also have the "_links" attribute, which is a collection of links, and with these you can access the car itself or get the owner of the car. To access one specific car, the path will be http://localhost:8080/api/cars/{id}.

The request to http://localhost:8080/api/cars/3/owner returns the owner of the car. The response now contains owner data, a link to the owner, and links to other cars that the user owns:

Spring Data Rest service provides all CRUD operations. The following table shows which HTTP methods you can use for different CRUD operations:

HTTP Method	CRUD
GET	Read
POST	Create
PUT/PATCH	Update
DELETE	Delete

Next, we will look at how to delete a car from the database by using our RESTful web service. In a delete operation, you have to use the DELETE method and the link to the car that will be deleted (`http://localhost:8080/api/cars/{id}`). The following screenshot shows how you can delete one car with the ID 4 by using cURL. After the delete request, you can see that there are now two cars left in the database:

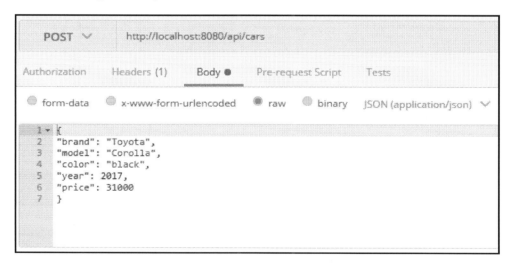

When we want to add a new car to the database, we have to use the POST method, and the link is `http://localhost:8080/api/cars`. The header must contain the **Content-Type** field with the value `Content-Type:application/json`, and the new car object will be embedded in the request body:

The response will send a newly created car object back. Now, if you again make a GET request to the `http://localhost:8080/api/cars` path, you can see that the new car exists in the database:

To update entities, we have to use the PATCH method and the link to the car that we want to update (`http://localhost:8080/api/cars/{id}`). The header must contain the **Content-Type** field with the value `Content-Type:application/json` and the car object, with edited data, will be given inside the request body. If you are using PATCH, you have to send only fields that are updates. If you are using PUT, you have to include all fields to request. Let's edit our car that we created in the previous example. We will change the color to white and fill in the register number that we left empty.

We will also link an owner to the car by using the owner field. The content of the owner field is the link to the owner (`http://localhost:8080/api/owners/{id}`). The following screenshot shows the PATCH request content:

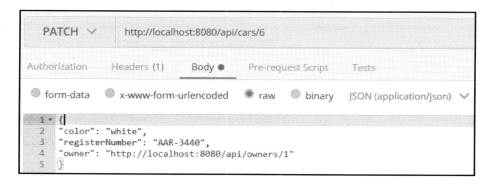

You can see that the car is updated after you fetch all cars by using GET request:

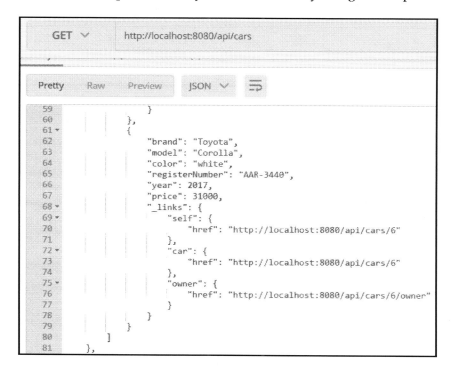

In the previous chapter, we created queries to our repository. These queries can also be included in our service. To include queries, you have to add the @RepositoryRestResource annotation to the repository class. Query parameters are annotated with the @Param annotation. The following source code shows our CarRepository with these annotations:

```
package com.packt.cardatabase.domain;

import java.util.List;

import org.springframework.data.repository.CrudRepository;
import org.springframework.data.repository.query.Param;
import org.springframework.data.rest.core.annotation.RepositoryRestResource;

@RepositoryRestResource
public interface CarRepository extends CrudRepository <Car, Long> {
  // Fetch cars by brand
  List<Car> findByBrand(@Param("brand") String brand);

  // Fetch cars by color
  List<Car> findByColor(@Param("color") String color);
}
```

Now, when you make a GET request to the http://localhost:8080/api/cars path, you can see that there is a new endpoint called /search. Calling the http://localhost:8080/api/cars/search path returns the following response:

From the response, you can see that both queries are now available in our service. The following URL demonstrates how to fetch cars by brand:

```
http://localhost:8080/api/cars/search/findByBrand?brand=Ford
```

```
GET ∨        http://localhost:8080/api/cars/search/findByBrand?brand=Ford

Pretty   Raw   Preview    JSON ∨    ⇥

1 ▾  {
2 ▾      "_embedded": {
3 ▾          "cars": [
4 ▾              {
5                   "brand": "Ford",
6                   "model": "Mustang",
7                   "color": "Red",
8                   "registerNumber": "ADF-1121",
9                   "year": 2017,
10                  "price": 59000,
11 ▾                "_links": {
12 ▾                    "self": {
13                          "href": "http://localhost:8080/api/cars/3"
14                      },
15 ▾                    "car": {
16                          "href": "http://localhost:8080/api/cars/3"
17                      },
18 ▾                    "owner": {
19                          "href": "http://localhost:8080/api/cars/3/owner"
20                      }
21                  }
22              }
23          ]
24      },
```

Summary

In this chapter, we created a RESTful web service with Spring Boot. First, we created a controller and one method that returns all cars in JSON format. Next, we used Spring Data REST to get a fully functional web service with all CRUD functionalities. We covered different types of requests that are needed to use CRUD functionalities of the service that we created. Finally, we also included our queries to service. In the next chapter we will secure our backend using Spring Security.

Questions

1. What is REST?
2. How can you create a RESTful web service with Spring Boot?
3. How can you fetch items using our RESTful web service?
4. How can you delete items using our RESTful web service?
5. How can you add items using our RESTful web service?
6. How can you update items using our RESTful web service?
7. How can you use queries with our RESTful web service?

Further reading

Pack has other great resources for learning about Spring Boot RESTful Web Services:

- https://www.packtpub.com/application-development/learning-spring-boot-20-second-edition
- https://www.packtpub.com/web-development/spring-boot-getting-started-integrated-course
- https://www.packtpub.com/web-development/building-restful-web-service-spring

4
Securing and Testing Your Backend

This chapter explains how to secure and test your Spring Boot backend. We will use the database application that we created in the previous chapter as a starting point.

In this chapter, we will look into the following:

- How to secure your Spring Boot backend with Spring Boot
- How to secure your Spring Boot backend with JWT
- How to test your backend

Technical requirements

The Spring Boot application that was created in previous chapters is necessary.

Spring Security

Spring Security (`https://spring.io/projects/spring-security`) provides security services for Java-based web applications. The Spring Security project started in 2003 and was previously named *The Acegi Security System for Spring*.

By default, Spring Security enables the following features:

- An `AuthenticationManager` bean with an in-memory single user. The username is `user` and the password is printed to the console output.
- Ignored paths for common static resource locations, such as `/css`, `/images`, and more.
- HTTP basic security for all other endpoints.
- Security events published to Spring `ApplicationEventPublisher`.
- Common low-level features are on by default (HSTS, XSS, CSRF, and so forth).

You can include Spring Security in your application by adding the following dependency to the `pom.xml` file:

```
<dependency>
    <groupId>org.springframework.boot</groupId>
    <artifactId>spring-boot-starter-security</artifactId>
</dependency>
```

When you start your application, you can see from the console that Spring Security has created an in-memory user with the username `user`. The user's password can be seen in the console output:

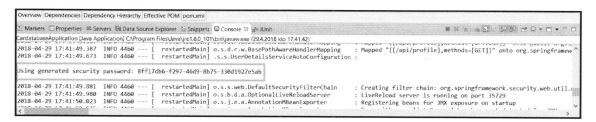

If you make a `GET` request to your API endpoint, you will see that it is now secure, and you will get a `401 Unauthorized` error:

To be able to make a successful GET request, we have to use basic authentication. The following screenshot shows how to do it with Postman. Now, with authentication we can see that status is **200 OK** and the response is sent:

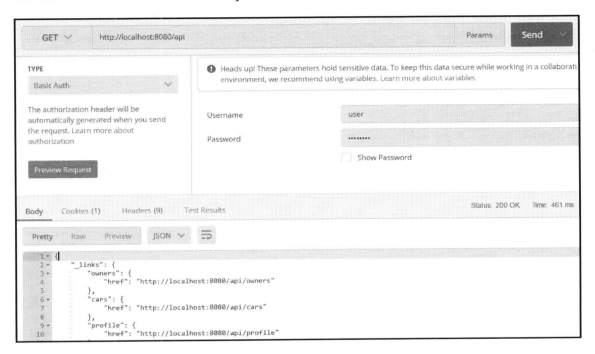

To configure how Spring Security behaves, we have to add a new configuration class that extends the WebSecurityConfigurerAdapter. Create a new class called SecurityConfig in your application root package. The following source code shows the structure of the security configuration class. The @Configuration and @EnableWebSecurity annotations switch off the default web security configuration and we can define our own configuration in this class. Inside the configure(HttpSecurity http) method, we can define which endpoints in our application are secured and which are not. We actually don't need this method yet because we can use the default settings where all endpoints are secured:

```
package com.packt.cardatabase;

import org.springframework.context.annotation.Configuration;
import
org.springframework.security.config.annotation.web.builders.HttpSecurity;
import
org.springframework.security.config.annotation.web.configuration.EnableWebS
```

```
ecurity;
import
org.springframework.security.config.annotation.web.configuration.WebSecurit
yConfigurerAdapter;

@Configuration
@EnableWebSecurity
public class SecurityConfig extends WebSecurityConfigurerAdapter {
  @Override
  protected void configure(HttpSecurity http) throws Exception {

  }

}
```

We also can add in-memory users to our application by adding
the `userDetailsService()` method into our `SecurityConfig` class. The following is the
source code of the method and it will create an in-memory user with the username
`user` and password `password`:

```
@Bean
@Override
public UserDetailsService userDetailsService() {
    UserDetails user =
        User.withDefaultPasswordEncoder()
            .username("user")
            .password("password")
            .roles("USER")
            .build();

    return new InMemoryUserDetailsManager(user);
}
```

The usage of in-memory users is good in the development phase, but the real application
should save the users in the database. To save the users to the database, you have to create
a user entity class and repository. Passwords shouldn't be saved to the database in plain
text format. Spring Security provides multiple hashing algorithms, such as BCrypt, that you
can use to hash passwords. The following steps show how to implement that:

1. Create a new class called `User` in the `domain` package. Activate the `domain`
   package and right click your mouse. Select **New | Class** from the menu and give
   the name `User` to a new class. After that, your project structure should look like
   the following screenshot:

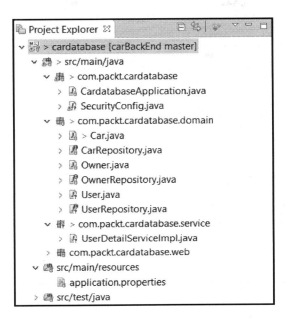

2. Annotate the `User` class with the `@Entity` annotation. Add the class fields—ID, username, password, and role. Finally, add the constructors, getters, and setters. We will set all fields to be nullable and that the username must be unique, by using the `@Column` annotation. See the following `User.java` source code of the fields and constructors:

```
package com.packt.cardatabase.domain;

import javax.persistence.Column;
import javax.persistence.Entity;
import javax.persistence.GeneratedValue;
import javax.persistence.GenerationType;
import javax.persistence.Id;

@Entity
public class User {
    @Id
    @GeneratedValue(strategy = GenerationType.IDENTITY)
    @Column(nullable = false, updatable = false)
    private Long id;

    @Column(nullable = false, unique = true)
    private String username;

    @Column(nullable = false)
```

```
    private String password;

    @Column(nullable = false)
    private String role;

    public User() {
    }
public User(String username, String password, String role) {
    super();
    this.username = username;
    this.password = password;
    this.role = role;
}
```

The following is the rest of the User.java source code with the getters and setters:

```
public Long getId() {
    return id;
}

public void setId(Long id) {
    this.id = id;
}

public String getUsername() {
    return username;
}

public void setUsername(String username) {
    this.username = username;
}

public String getPassword() {
    return password;
}

public void setPassword(String password) {
    this.password = password;
}

public String getRole() {
    return role;
}

public void setRole(String role) {
    this.role = role;
```

```
    }
}
```

3. Create a new class called `UserRepository` in the `domain` package. Activate the `domain` package and right click your mouse. Select **New | Class** from the menu and give the name `UserRepository` to the new class.

4. The source code of the repository class is similar to what we have done in the previous chapter, but there is one query method, `findByUsername`, that we need in the next steps. See the following `UserRepository` source code:

```java
package com.packt.cardatabase.domain;

import org.springframework.data.repository.CrudRepository;
import org.springframework.stereotype.Repository;

@Repository
public interface UserRepository extends CrudRepository<User, Long>
{
    User findByUsername(String username);
}
```

5. Next, we create a class that implements the `UserDetailsService` interface provided by Spring Security. Spring Security uses this for user authentication and authorization. Create a new package in the root package called `service`. Activate the root package and right click your mouse. Select **New | Package** from the menu and give the name `service` to a new package:

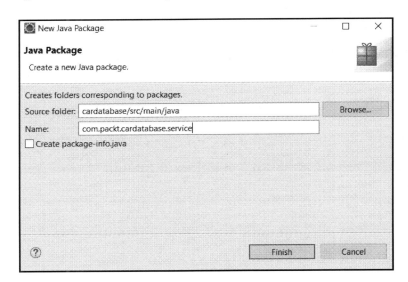

6. Create a new class called `UserDetailServiceImpl` in the `service` package we just created. Now your project structure should look like the following:

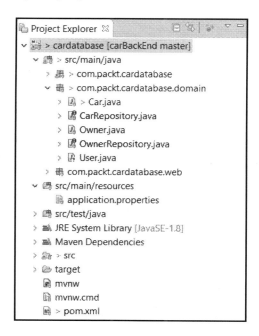

7. We have to inject the `UserRepository` class into the `UserDetailServiceImpl` class because that is needed to fetch the user from the database when Spring Security handles authentication.
   The `loadByUsername` method returns the `UserDetails` object, which is needed for authentication. Following is the source code of `UserDetailServiceImpl.java`:

```
package com.packt.cardatabase.service;

import org.springframework.beans.factory.annotation.Autowired;
import org.springframework.security.core.authority.AuthorityUtils;
import org.springframework.security.core.userdetails.UserDetails;
import
org.springframework.security.core.userdetails.UserDetailsService;
import
org.springframework.security.core.userdetails.UsernameNotFoundExcep
tion;
import org.springframework.stereotype.Service;

import com.packt.cardatabase.domain.User;
```

```
import com.packt.cardatabase.domain.UserRepository;

@Service
public class UserDetailServiceImpl implements UserDetailsService {
  @Autowired
  private UserRepository repository;


    @Override
    public UserDetails loadUserByUsername(String username) throws
UsernameNotFoundException
    {
      User currentUser = repository.findByUsername(username);
        UserDetails user = new org.springframework.security.core
            .userdetails.User(username, currentUser.getPassword()
            , true, true, true, true,
AuthorityUtils.createAuthorityList(currentUser.getRole()));
        return user;
    }
}
```

8. In our security configuration class, we have to define that Spring Security should use users from the database instead of in-memory users. Delete the userDetailsService() method from the SecurityConfig class to disable in-memory users. Add a new configureGlobal method to enable users from the database. We shouldn't ever save the password as plain text to the database. Therefore, we will define a password hashing algorithm in the configureGlobal method. In this example, we are using the BCrypt algorithm. This can be easily implemented with the Spring Security BCryptPasswordEncoder class. Following is the SecurityConfig.java source code. Now, the password must be hashed using BCrypt before it's saved to the database:

```
package com.packt.cardatabase;

import org.springframework.beans.factory.annotation.Autowired;
import org.springframework.context.annotation.Configuration;
import
org.springframework.security.config.annotation.authentication.build
ers.AuthenticationManagerBuilder;
import
org.springframework.security.config.annotation.web.builders.HttpSec
urity;
import
org.springframework.security.config.annotation.web.configuration.En
ableWebSecurity;
```

```
import
org.springframework.security.config.annotation.web.configuration.We
bSecurityConfigurerAdapter;
import
org.springframework.security.crypto.bcrypt.BCryptPasswordEncoder;

import com.packt.cardatabase.service.UserDetailServiceImpl;

@Configuration
@EnableWebSecurity
public class SecurityConfig extends WebSecurityConfigurerAdapter {
  @Autowired
  private UserDetailServiceImpl userDetailsService;

  @Autowired
  public void configureGlobal(AuthenticationManagerBuilder auth)
throws Exception {
    auth.userDetailsService(userDetailsService)
    .passwordEncoder(new BCryptPasswordEncoder());
  }
}
```

9. Finally, we can save a couple of test users to the database in our `CommandLineRunner`. Open the `CardatabaseApplication.java` file and add following code at the beginning of the class to inject `UserRepository` into the main class:

```
@Autowired
private UserRepository urepository;
```

10. Save the users to the database with hashed passwords. You can use any BCrypt calculator found on the internet:

```
@Bean
CommandLineRunner runner() {
  return args -> {
    Owner owner1 = new Owner("John" , "Johnson");
    Owner owner2 = new Owner("Mary" , "Robinson");
    orepository.save(owner1);
    orepository.save(owner2);
    repository.save(new Car("Ford", "Mustang", "Red", "ADF-1121",
      2017, 59000, owner1));
    repository.save(new Car("Nissan", "Leaf", "White", "SSJ-3002",
      2014, 29000, owner2));
    repository.save(new Car("Toyota", "Prius", "Silver", "KKO-0212",
      2018, 39000, owner2));
```

```
// username: user password: user
urepository.save(new User("user",
"$2a$04$1.YhMIgNX/8TkCKGFUONWO1waedKhQ5KrnB30f1OQ01QKqmzLf.Zi",
"USER"));
// username: admin password: admin
urepository.save(new User("admin",
"$2a$04$KNLUwOWHVQZVpXyMBNc7JOzbLiBjb9Tk9bP7KNcPI12ICuvzXQQKG",
"ADMIN"));
};
}
```

After running your application, you see that there is now a `user` table in the database and two user records are saved:

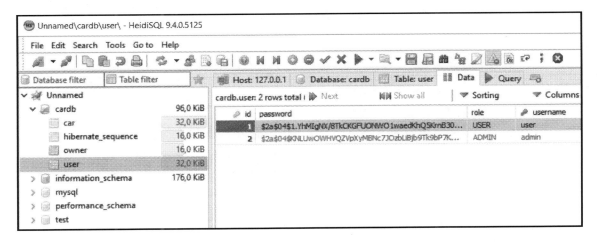

Now, you will get a `401 Unauthorized` error if you try to send a `GET` request to the `/api` endpoint without authentication. You should authenticate to be able to send a successful request. The difference to the previous example is that we are using the users from the database to authenticate.

You can see a GET request to the /api endpoint using the admin user in the following screenshot:

```
 root@HHMX4717: ~
root@HHMX4717:~# curl http://localhost:8080/api -u admin
Enter host password for user 'admin':
{
  "_links" : {
    "owners" : {
      "href" : "http://localhost:8080/api/owners"
    },
    "users" : {
      "href" : "http://localhost:8080/api/users"
    },
    "cars" : {
      "href" : "http://localhost:8080/api/cars"
    },
    "profile" : {
      "href" : "http://localhost:8080/api/profile"
    }
  }
}root@HHMX4717:~#
```

Securing your backend using JWT

In the previous section, we covered how to use basic authentication with the RESTful web service. That is not usable when we are going to develop our own frontend with React. We are going to use the **JSON Web Tokens (JWT)** authentication in our application. JWT is a compact way to implement authentication in modern web applications. JWT is really small in size and therefore it can be sent in the URL, in the POST parameter, or inside the header. It also contains all required information about the user.

The JSON web token contains three different parts separated by dots. The first part is the header that defines the type of the token and the hashing algorithm. The second part is the payload that, typically, in the case of authentication, contains information about the user. The third part is the signature that is used to verify that the token hasn't been changed along the way. You can see the following example of a JWT token:

```
eyJhbGciOiJIUzI1NiJ9.
eyJzdWIiOiJKb2UifD.
ipevRNuRP6HflG8cFKnmUPtypruRC4fc1DWtoLL62SY
```

The following diagram shows the main idea of the JWT authentication process:

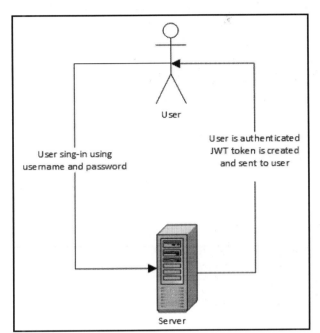

After successful authentication, the requests sent by the user should always contain the JWT token that was received in the authentication.

We will use the Java JWT library (`https://github.com/jwtk/jjwt`), which is the JSON Web Token library for Java and Android; therefore, we have to add the following dependency to the `pom.xml` file. The JWT library is used for creating and parsing JWT tokens:

```
<dependency>
  <groupId>io.jsonwebtoken</groupId>
  <artifactId>jjwt</artifactId>
  <version>0.9.0</version>
</dependency>
```

The following steps show how to enable JWT authentication in our backend:

1. Create a new class called `AuthenticationService` in the `service` package. In the beginning of the class we will define a few constants; `EXPIRATIONTIME` defines the expiration time of the token in milliseconds. `SIGNINGKEY` is an algorithm-specific signing key used to digitally sign the JWT. You should use a base64 encoded string. PREFIX defines the prefix of the token and the Bearer schema is typically used. The `addToken` method creates the token and adds it to the request's `Authorization` header. The signing key is encoded using the SHA-512 algorithm. The method also adds `Access-Control-Expose-Headers` to the header with the `Authorization` value. This is needed because we are not able to access the `Authorization` header through a JavaScript frontend by default. The `getAuthentication` method gets the token from the response `Authorization` header using the `parser()` method provided by the `jjwt` library. The whole `AuthenticationService` source code can be seen here:

```
package com.packt.cardatabase.service;

import io.jsonwebtoken.Jwts;
import io.jsonwebtoken.SignatureAlgorithm;
import
org.springframework.security.authentication.UsernamePasswordAuthent
icationToken;
import org.springframework.security.core.Authentication;

import javax.servlet.http.HttpServletRequest;
import javax.servlet.http.HttpServletResponse;
import java.util.Date;

import static java.util.Collections.emptyList;

public class AuthenticationService {
  static final long EXPIRATIONTIME = 864_000_00; // 1 day in
milliseconds
  static final String SIGNINGKEY = "SecretKey";
  static final String PREFIX = "Bearer";

  // Add token to Authorization header
  static public void addToken(HttpServletResponse res, String
username) {
    String JwtToken = Jwts.builder().setSubject(username)
      .setExpiration(new Date(System.currentTimeMillis()
        + EXPIRATIONTIME))
      .signWith(SignatureAlgorithm.HS512, SIGNINGKEY)
      .compact();
```

```
    res.addHeader("Authorization", PREFIX + " " + JwtToken);
    res.addHeader("Access-Control-Expose-Headers", "Authorization");
  }

  // Get token from Authorization header
  static public Authentication getAuthentication(HttpServletRequest
request) {
    String token = request.getHeader("Authorization");
    if (token != null) {
      String user = Jwts.parser()
          .setSigningKey(SIGNINGKEY)
          .parseClaimsJws(token.replace(PREFIX, ""))
          .getBody()
          .getSubject();

      if (user != null)
        return new UsernamePasswordAuthenticationToken(user, null,
            emptyList());
    }
    return null;
  }
}
```

2. Next, we will add a new simple POJO class to keep credentials for authentication. Create a new class called `AccountCredentials` in the `domain` package. The class has two fields—`username` and `password`. The following is the source code of the class. This class doesn't have the `@Entity` annotation because we don't have to save credentials to the database:

```
package com.packt.cardatabase.domain;

public class AccountCredentials {
  private String username;
  private String password;
  public String getUsername() {
    return username;
  }
  public void setUsername(String username) {
    this.username = username;
  }
  public String getPassword() {
    return password;
  }
  public void setPassword(String password) {
    this.password = password;
  }
}
```

3. We will use filter classes for login and authentication. Create a new class called `LoginFilter` in the root package that handles `POST` requests to the `/login` endpoint. The `LoginFilter` class extends the Spring Security `AbstractAuthenticationProcessingFilter`, which requires that you set the `authenticationManager` property. Authentication is performed by the `attemptAuthentication` method. If the authentication is successful, the `succesfulAuthentication` method is executed. This method will then call the `addToken` method in our service class and the token will be added to the `Authorization` header:

```java
package com.packt.cardatabase;

import java.io.IOException;
import java.util.Collections;

import javax.servlet.FilterChain;
import javax.servlet.ServletException;
import javax.servlet.http.HttpServletRequest;
import javax.servlet.http.HttpServletResponse;

import
org.springframework.security.authentication.AuthenticationManager;
import
org.springframework.security.authentication.UsernamePasswordAuthent
icationToken;
import org.springframework.security.core.Authentication;
import org.springframework.security.core.AuthenticationException;
import
org.springframework.security.web.authentication.AbstractAuthenticat
ionProcessingFilter;
import
org.springframework.security.web.util.matcher.AntPathRequestMatcher
;

import com.fasterxml.jackson.databind.ObjectMapper;
import com.packt.cardatabase.domain.AccountCredentials;
import com.packt.cardatabase.service.AuthenticationService;

public class LoginFilter extends
AbstractAuthenticationProcessingFilter {

  public LoginFilter(String url, AuthenticationManager authManager)
{
    super(new AntPathRequestMatcher(url));
    setAuthenticationManager(authManager);
  }
```

```
@Override
public Authentication attemptAuthentication(
HttpServletRequest req, HttpServletResponse res)
    throws AuthenticationException, IOException, ServletException
{
AccountCredentials creds = new ObjectMapper()
    .readValue(req.getInputStream(), AccountCredentials.class);
return getAuthenticationManager().authenticate(
    new UsernamePasswordAuthenticationToken(
        creds.getUsername(),
        creds.getPassword(),
        Collections.emptyList()
    )
  );
}

@Override
protected void successfulAuthentication(
    HttpServletRequest req,
    HttpServletResponse res, FilterChain chain,
    Authentication auth) throws IOException, ServletException {
  AuthenticationService.addToken(res, auth.getName());
}
}
```

4. Create a new class called `AuthenticationFilter` in the root package. The class extends `GenericFilterBean`, which is a generic superclass for any type of filter. This class will handle authentication in all other endpoints except `/login`. The `AuthenticationFilter` uses the `addAuthentication` method from our service class to get a token from the request `Authorization` header:

```
package com.packt.cardatabase;

import java.io.IOException;

import javax.servlet.FilterChain;
import javax.servlet.ServletException;
import javax.servlet.ServletRequest;
import javax.servlet.ServletResponse;
import javax.servlet.http.HttpServletRequest;

import org.springframework.security.core.Authentication;
import
org.springframework.security.core.context.SecurityContextHolder;
import org.springframework.web.filter.GenericFilterBean;

import com.packt.cardatabase.service.AuthenticationService;
```

```
public class AuthenticationFilter extends GenericFilterBean {
  @Override
  public void doFilter(ServletRequest request, ServletResponse
response, FilterChain filterChain) throws IOException,
ServletException {
    Authentication authentication =
AuthenticationService.getAuthentication((HttpServletRequest)request
);
    SecurityContextHolder.getContext().
       setAuthentication(authentication);
    filterChain.doFilter(request, response);
  }
}
```

5. Finally, we have to make changes to our `SecurityConfig` class's `configure` method. There, we define that the POST method request to the `/login` endpoint is allowed without authentication and that requests to all other endpoints need authentication. We also define the filters to be used in the `/login` and other endpoints by using the `addFilterBefore` method:

```
//SecurityConfig.java
@Override
  protected void configure(HttpSecurity http) throws Exception {
    http.cors().and().authorizeRequests()
      .antMatchers(HttpMethod.POST, "/login").permitAll()
        .anyRequest().authenticated()
        .and()
        // Filter for the api/login requests
        .addFilterBefore(new LoginFilter("/login",
         authenticationManager()),
                UsernamePasswordAuthenticationFilter.class)
        // Filter for other requests to check JWT in header
        .addFilterBefore(new AuthenticationFilter(),
                UsernamePasswordAuthenticationFilter.class);
  }
```

6. We will also add a **CORS (Cross-Origin Resource Sharing)** filter in our security configuration class. This is needed for the frontend, that is sending requests from the other origin. The CORS filter intercepts requests, and if these are identified as cross origin, it adds proper headers to the request. For that, we will use Spring Security's `CorsConfigurationSource` interface. In this example, we will allow all HTTP methods and headers. You can define the list of allowed origins, methods, and headers here, if you need more finely graded definition. Add the following source into your `SecurityConfig` class to enable the CORS filter:

```java
// SecurityConfig.java
@Bean
  CorsConfigurationSource corsConfigurationSource() {
      UrlBasedCorsConfigurationSource source =
          new UrlBasedCorsConfigurationSource();
      CorsConfiguration config = new CorsConfiguration();
      config.setAllowedOrigins(Arrays.asList("*"));
      config.setAllowedMethods(Arrays.asList("*"));
      config.setAllowedHeaders(Arrays.asList("*"));
      config.setAllowCredentials(true);
      config.applyPermitDefaultValues();
      source.registerCorsConfiguration("/**", config);
      return source;
}
```

Now, after you run the application, we can call the `/login` endpoint with the `POST` method and, in the case of a successful login, we will receive a JWT token in the `Authorization` header:

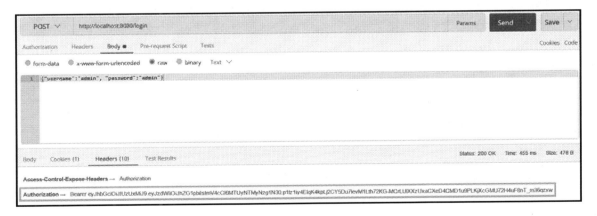

After successful login, we can call the other RESTful service endpoints by sending the JWT token received from the login in the `Authorization` header. See the example in the following screenshot:

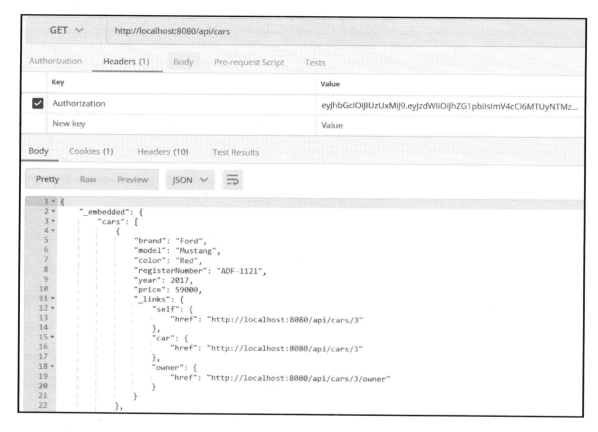

Now, all the functionalities that are needed have been implemented to our backend. Next, we will continue with backend unit testing.

Testing in Spring Boot

The Spring Boot test starter package is added to `pom.xml` by Spring Initializr when we created our project. That is added automatically without any selection in the Spring Initializr page:

```
<dependency>
    <groupId>org.springframework.boot</groupId>
    <artifactId>spring-boot-starter-test</artifactId>
    <scope>test</scope>
</dependency>
```

The Spring Boot test starter provides lot of handy libraries for testing, such as JUnit, Mockito, AssertJ, and more. If you look, your project structure already has its own package created for test classes:

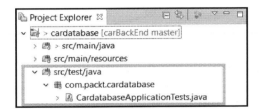

By default, Spring Boot uses an in-memory database for testing. We are now using MariaDB, but H2 can also be used for testing by adding the following dependency to the `pom.xml` file. The scope defines that the H2 database will be used only for running tests; otherwise, the application will use the MariaDB database:

```
<dependency>
    <groupId>com.h2database</groupId>
    <artifactId>h2</artifactId>
    <scope>test</scope>
</dependency>
```

If you also want to use the default database for testing, you can use the `@AutoConfigureTestDatabase` annotation.

Creating unit tests

For unit testing, we are using a JUnit, which is a popular Java-based unit testing library. The following source code shows the example skeleton of the Spring Boot test class. The @SpringBootTest annotation specifies that the class is a regular test class that runs Spring Boot based tests. The @Test annotation before the method defines to JUnit that the method can be run as a test case. The @RunWith(SpringRunner.class) annotation provides Spring ApplicationContext and get beans injected into your test instance:

```
@RunWith(SpringRunner.class)
@SpringBootTest
public class MyTestsClass {

   @Test
   public void testMethod() {
      ...
   }

}
```

First, we will create our first test case, which will test the major functionality of your application before creating any formal test cases. Open the CardatabaseApplicationTest test class that has already been made for your application. There is one test method called contextLoads where we will add the test. The following test checks that the instance of controller was created and injected successfully:

```
package com.packt.cardatabase;

import static org.assertj.core.api.Assertions.assertThat;

import org.junit.Test;
import org.junit.runner.RunWith;
import org.springframework.beans.factory.annotation.Autowired;
import org.springframework.boot.test.context.SpringBootTest;
import org.springframework.test.context.junit4.SpringRunner;

import com.packt.cardatabase.web.CarController;

@RunWith(SpringRunner.class)
@SpringBootTest
public class CardatabaseApplicationTests {
   @Autowired
   private CarController controller;

   @Test
   public void contextLoads() {
```

```
            assertThat(controller).isNotNull();
   }

}
```

To run tests in Eclipse, activate the test class in the **Project Explorer** and right-click your mouse. Select **Run As | JUnit test** from the menu. You should now see the **JUnit** tab in the lower part of the Eclipse workbench. The test results are shown in this tab and the test case has been passed:

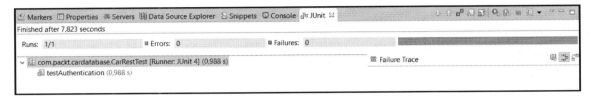

Next, we will create unit tests for our car repository to test CRUD operations. Create a new class called `CarRepositoryTest` in the root test package. Instead of the `@SpringBootTest` annotation, the `@DataJpaTest` can be used if the test focuses only on JPA components. When using this annotation the H2 database, Hibernate, and Spring Data are configured automatically for testing. SQL logging will be also turned on. The tests are transactional by default and roll back at the end of the test case. `TestEntityManager` is used to handle the persist entities and it is designed to be used in testing. You can see in the following, the source code of the JPA test class skeleton:

```java
package com.packt.cardatabase;

import static org.assertj.core.api.Assertions.assertThat;

import org.junit.Test;
import org.junit.runner.RunWith;
import org.springframework.beans.factory.annotation.Autowired;
import org.springframework.boot.test.autoconfigure.orm.jpa.DataJpaTest;
import
org.springframework.boot.test.autoconfigure.orm.jpa.TestEntityManager;
import org.springframework.test.context.junit4.SpringRunner;

import com.packt.cardatabase.domain.Car;
import com.packt.cardatabase.domain.CarRepository;

@RunWith(SpringRunner.class)
@DataJpaTest
public class CarRepositoryTest {
  @Autowired
```

```
    private TestEntityManager entityManager;
    @Autowired
    private CarRepository repository;
     // Test cases..
}
```

We will add out first test case to test the addition of a new car to database. A new `car` object is created and saved to the database with the `persistAndFlush` method provided by `TestEntityManager`. Then, we check that the car ID cannot be null if it is saved successfully. The following source code shows the test case method. Add the following method code into your `CarRepositoryTest` class:

```
@Test
public void saveCar() {
   Car car = new Car("Tesla", "Model X", "White", "ABC-1234",
       2017, 86000);
   entityManager.persistAndFlush(car);
   assertThat(car.getId()).isNotNull();
}
```

The second test case will test the deletion of cars from the database. A new `car` object is created and saved to the database. Then, all cars are deleted from the database, and finally, the `findAll()` query method should return an empty list. The following source code shows the test case method. Add the following method code into your `CarRepositoryTest` class:

```
@Test
public void deleteCars() {
   entityManager.persistAndFlush(new Car("Tesla", "Model X", "White",
       "ABC-1234", 2017, 86000));
   entityManager.persistAndFlush(new Car("Mini", "Cooper", "Yellow",
       "BWS-3007", 2015, 24500));
   repository.deleteAll();
   assertThat(repository.findAll()).isEmpty();
}
```

Run the test cases and check on the Eclipse **JUnit** tab that the tests were passed:

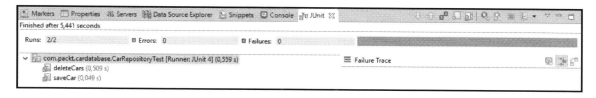

Next, we will show how to test your RESTful web service JWT authentication functionality. For testing the controllers or any endpoint that is exposed, we can use a MockMvc. By using the MockMvc, the server is not started but the tests are performed in the layer where Spring handles HTTP requests, and therefore it mocks the real situation. MockMvc provides the perform method to send the requests. To test authentication, we have to add credentials to the request body. We perform two requests; the first has the correct credentials and we check that the status is **OK**. The second request contains incorrect credentials and we check that we get a 4XX HTTP error:

```
package com.packt.cardatabase;

import static
org.springframework.test.web.servlet.request.MockMvcRequestBuilders.post;
import static
org.springframework.test.web.servlet.result.MockMvcResultHandlers.print;
import static
org.springframework.test.web.servlet.result.MockMvcResultMatchers.status;

import org.junit.Test;
import org.junit.runner.RunWith;
import org.springframework.beans.factory.annotation.Autowired;
import
org.springframework.boot.test.autoconfigure.web.servlet.AutoConfigureMockMv
c;
import org.springframework.boot.test.context.SpringBootTest;

import org.springframework.test.context.junit4.SpringRunner;
import org.springframework.test.web.servlet.MockMvc;

@RunWith(SpringRunner.class)
@SpringBootTest
@AutoConfigureMockMvc
public class CarRestTest {
  @Autowired
    private MockMvc mockMvc;
  @Test
  public void testAuthentication() throws Exception {
    // Testing authentication with correct credentials
      this.mockMvc.perform(post("/login")
        .content("{\"username\":\"admin\", \"password\":\"admin\"}")).
        andDo(print()).andExpect(status().isOk());

    // Testing authentication with wrong credentials
      this.mockMvc.perform(post("/login")
        .content("{\"username\":\"admin\", \"password\":\"wrongpwd\"}")).
        andDo(print()).andExpect(status().is4xxClientError());
```

```
      }

   }
```

Now, when we run the authentication tests, we can see that the test passed:

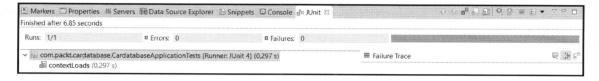

Now, we have covered the basics of testing in the Spring Boot application, and you should have the knowledge required to implement more test cases for your application.

Summary

In this chapter, we focused on securing and testing the Spring Boot backend. Securing was first done with Spring Security. The frontend will be developed with React in upcoming chapters; therefore, we implemented JWT authentication, which is a lightweight authentication method suitable for our needs. We also covered the basics of testing a Spring Boot application. We used JUnit for unit testing and implemented test cases for JPA and RESTful web service authentication. In the next chapter, we will setup the environment and tools for the frontend development.

Questions

1. What is Spring Security?
2. How can you secure your backend with Spring Boot?
3. What is JWT?
4. How can you secure your backend with JWT?
5. How can you create unit tests with Spring Boot?
6. How can you run and check the results of unit tests?

Further reading

Packt has other great resources for learning about Spring Security and Testing:

- https://www.packtpub.com/application-development/spring-security-third-edition
- https://www.packtpub.com/web-development/mastering-software-testing-junit-5

Setting Up the Environment and Tools – Frontend

This chapter describes the development environment and tools that are needed with React. This chapter is needed to be able to start frontend development. We will create a simple starter React app by using the Create React App starter kit made by Facebook.

In this chapter, we will look into the following:

- Installing Node.js and VS Code
- Creating a React.js app using `create-react-app`
- Running a React.js app
- Installing React Developer Tools

Technical requirements

In this book, we are using the Windows operating system, but all tools are available for Linux and macOS as well.

Installing Node.js

Node.js is an open source JavaScript-based server side environment. Node.js is available for multiple operating systems, such as Windows, macOS, and Linux. Node.js is needed to develop React apps.

The Node.js installation package can be found at `https://nodejs.org/en/download/`. Download the latest **Long-term Support (LTS)** version for your operating system. In this book, we are using the Windows 10 operating system and you can get the Node.js MSI installer for it, which makes installation really straightforward. When you execute the installer, you will go through the installation wizard and you can do so using the default settings:

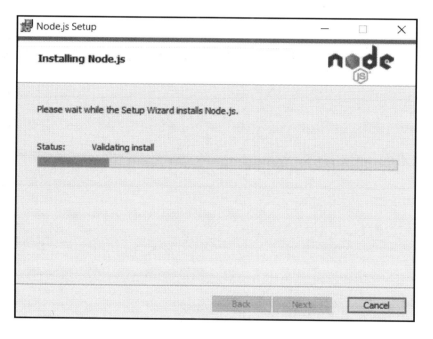

After the installation has been completed, we can check that everything went correctly. Open PowerShell, or whatever Terminal you are using, and type the following commands:

```
node -v
```

```
npm -v
```

The commands should show you the installed versions, Node.js and npm:

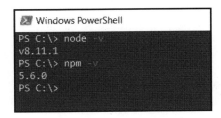

npm comes with the Node.js installation and is a package manager for JavaScript. We will use that a lot in the next chapters when we are installing different node modules to our React app. There is also another package manager called Yarn that you can use, as well.

Installing VS Code

Visual Studio Code (VS Code) is an open source code editor for multiple programming languages. VS Code is developed by Microsoft. There are a lot of different code editors available, such as Atom, Brackets, and others, and you can use something other than VS Code if you are familiar with it. VS Code is available for Windows, macOS, and Linux and you can download it from `https://code.visualstudio.com/`.

Installation for Windows is done with the MSI installer and you can do the installation with default settings. The following screenshot shows the workbench of VS Code. On the left side is the activity bar, which you can use to navigate between different views. Next to the activity bar is a side bar, which contains different views, such as project file explorer.

The editor takes up the rest of the workbench:

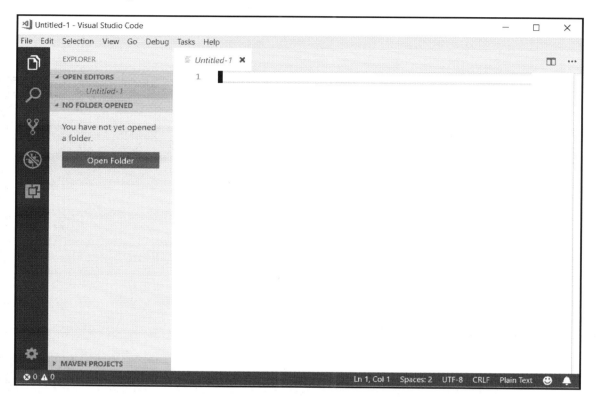

VS Code also has an integrated terminal that you can use to create and run React apps. The terminal can be found in the **View** | **Integrated Terminal** menu. You can also use this in later chapters when we create more React apps.

There are a lot of extensions available for different languages and frameworks. If you open **Extension Manager** from the activity bar, you can search for different extensions. One really handy extension for React development is **Reactjs Code Snippets**, which we recommend installing. It has multiple code snippets available for the React.js app, which make your development process faster. We will show you later how to use that extension. This is just one of many useful extensions and you should explore more extensions that might makes your life easier. For example, the **ESLint** extension helps you to find typos and syntax errors quickly and makes the formatting of the source code easier:

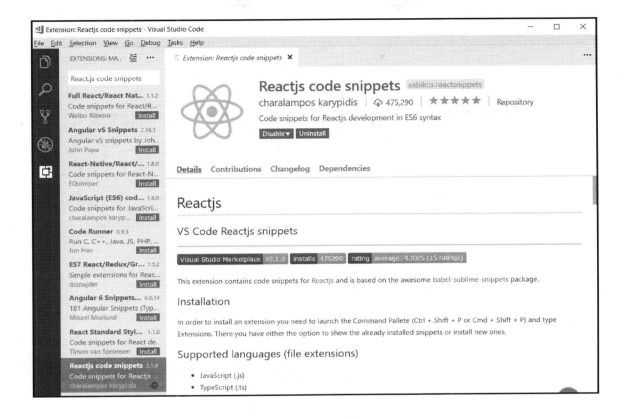

Creating and running a React app

When we have Node.js and the code editor installed, we are ready to create our first React.js app. We are using Facebook's `create-react-app` (https://github.com/facebook/create-react-app) for that. Here are the steps to make your first app:

1. Open PowerShell or the command-line tool and type the following command. The command installs the `create-react-app` starter, which we will use to develop React apps. Parameter `-g` in the command means that installation is done globally.

    If you are using npm version 5.2 or higher, you can also use npx instead of npm:

    ```
    npm install -g create-react-app
    ```

2. After the installation is complete, we create our first app by typing the following command:

```
create-react-app myapp
```

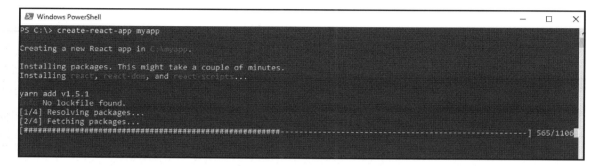

3. After the app has been created, move it into your `app` folder:

```
cd myapp
```

4. Then we can run the app with the following command. The command runs the app in port `3000` and opens the app in a browser:

```
npm start
```

5. Now your app is running and you should see the following page in a browser. The `npm start` command starts the app in development mode:

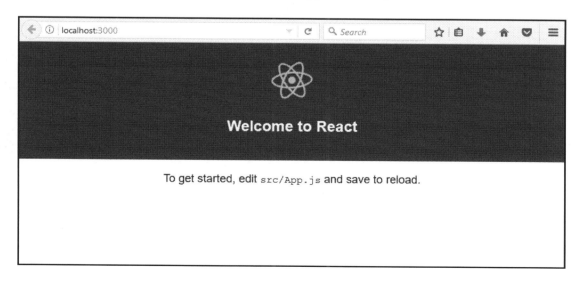

You can stop the development server by pressing *Ctrl + C* in PowerShell.

To build a minified version of your app for production, you can use the `npm run build` command, which builds your app in the `build` folder.

Modifying a React app

Open your React app folder with VS Code by selecting **File | Open folder**. You should see the app structure in the file explorer. The most important folder in this phase is the `src` folder, which contains the JavaScript source codes:

Open the `App.js` file from the `src` folder in the code editor. Remove the line that shows the image and save the file. You don't need to know anything more about this file, yet. We will go deeper into this topic in the next chapter:

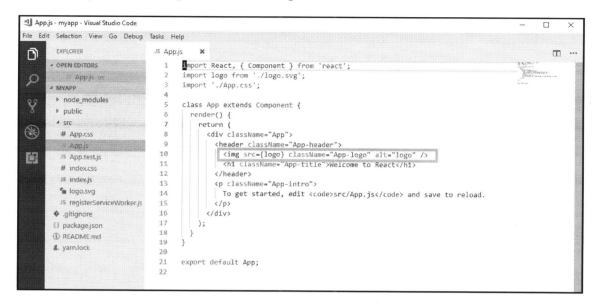

Now, if you look at the browser, you should see immediately that the image has disappeared from the page:

To debug React apps, we should also install React Developer Tools, which are available for Chrome or Firefox browsers. Chrome plugins can be installed from the Chrome Web Store (`https://chrome.google.com/webstore/category/extensions`) and Firefox add-ons from the Firefox add-ons site (`https://addons.mozilla.org`). After you have installed the React Developer Tools, you should see a new **React** tab in your browser's developer tools after you navigate to your React app. The following screenshot shows the developer tools in the Chrome browser:

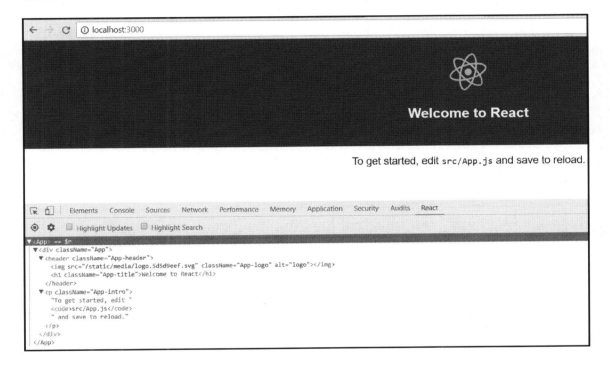

Summary

In this chapter, we installed everything that is needed to start our frontend development with React.js. First, we installed the Node.js and VS Code editor. Then we used the `create-react-app` starter kit to create our first React.js app. Finally, we ran the app and demonstrated how to modify it. This is just an overview of the app structure and modification, and we will continue this in the following chapters.

Questions

1. What is Node.js and npm?
2. How do you install Node.js?
3. What is VS Code?
4. How do you install VS Code?
5. How do you create a React.js app with `create-react-app`?
6. How do you run a React.js app?
7. How do you make basic modifications to your app?

Further reading

Packt has other great resources for learning about React:

- `https://www.packtpub.com/web-development/getting-started-react`
- `https://www.packtpub.com/web-development/react-16-tooling`

6
Getting Started with React

This chapter describes the basics of React programming. We will cover the skills that are needed to create basic functionalities for the React frontend. In JavaScript, we use the ES6 syntax because it provides many features that make coding cleaner.

In this chapter, we will look at the following:

- How to create React components
- How to use state and props in components
- Useful ES6 features
- What JSX is
- How to handle events and forms in React

Technical requirements

In this book, we are using the Windows operating system, but all tools are available for Linux and macOS as well.

Basic React components

According to Facebook, React is a JavaScript library for user interfaces. Since version 15, React has been developed under the MIT license. React is component-based and the components are independent and reusable. The components are basic building blocks of React. When you start to develop a user interface with React, it is good to start by creating a mock interfaces. That way, it is easy to identify what kind of components you have to create and how they interact.

From the following diagram of the mock, we can see how the user interface can be split into components. In this case, there will be an application root component, a search bar component, a table component, and a table row component:

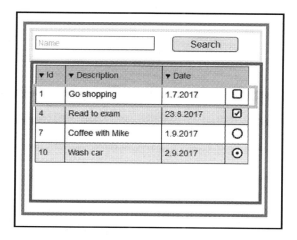

The components can then be arranged in the following tree hierarchy. The important thing to understand with React is that the dataflow is going from the parent component to the child:

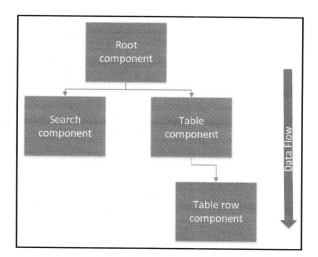

React uses the Virtual DOM for selective re-rendering of the user interface, which makes it more cost effective. The Virtual DOM is a lightweight copy of the DOM and manipulation of the virtual DOM is much faster than the real DOM. After the virtual DOM is updated, React compares it to a snapshot that has been taken from the virtual DOM before updates have been run. After the comparison, React knows which parts have been changed and only these parts are updated to the real DOM.

The React component can be defined by using a JavaScript function or the ES6 JavaScript class. We will go more deeply into ES6 in the next section. The following is a simple component source code that renders the Hello World text. The first code block uses the JavaScript function:

```
// Using JavaScript function
function Hello() {
  return <h1>Hello World</h1>;
}
```

And this one is uses the class to create a component:

```
// Using ES6 class
class Hello extends React.Component {
  render() {
    return <h1>Hello World</h1>;
  }
}
```

The component that was implemented using the class, contains the required render() method. This method shows and updates the rendered output of the component. The name of the user-defined component should start with a capital letter.

Let's make changes to our component's render method and a add new header element into it:

```
class App extends Component {
  render() {
    return (
      <h1>Hello World!</h1>
      <h2>From my first React app</h2>
    );
  }
}
```

When you run the app, you get the **Adjacent JSX elements must be wrapped in an enclosing tag** error. To fix this error, we have to wrap the headers in one element, such as div; since React version 16.2, we can also use Fragments, which look like empty JSX tags:

```
// Wrap headers in div
class App extends Component {
  render() {
    return (
      <div>
        <h1>Hello World!</h1>
        <h2>From my first React app</h2>
      </div>
    );
  }
}

// Or using fragments
class App extends Component {
  render() {
    return (
      <>
        <h1>Hello World!</h1>
        <h2>From my first React app</h2>
      </>
    );
  }
}
```

Let's look more carefully at the first React app that we created in the previous chapter using create-react-app. The source code of the Index.js file in the root folder looks as follows:

```
import React from 'react';
import ReactDOM from 'react-dom';
import './index.css';
import App from './App';
import registerServiceWorker from './registerServiceWorker';

ReactDOM.render(<App />, document.getElementById('root'));
registerServiceWorker();
```

At the beginning of the file, there are `import` statements that load components or assets to our file. For example, the second line imports the `react-dom` package from the `node_modules` folder, and the fourth line imports the `App` (the `App.js` file in the root folder) component. The `react-dom` package provides DOM-specific methods for us. To render the React component to the DOM, we can use the `render` method from the `react-dom` package. The first argument is the component that will be rendered and the second argument is the element or container where the component will be rendered. In this case, the `root` element is `<div id="root"></div>`, which can be found in the `index.html` file inside the `public` folder. See the following `index.html` file:

```html
<!DOCTYPE html>
<html lang="en">
  <head>
    <meta charset="utf-8">
    <meta name="viewport" content="width=device-width, initial-scale=1,
      shrink-to-fit=no">
    <meta name="theme-color" content="#000000">

    <link rel="manifest" href="%PUBLIC_URL%/manifest.json">
    <link rel="shortcut icon" href="%PUBLIC_URL%/favicon.ico">

    <title>React App</title>
  </head>
  <body>
    <div id="root"></div>
  </body>
</html>
```

The following source code shows the `App.js` component from our first React app. You can see that `import` applies also to assets, such as images and style sheets. At the end of the source code, there is an `export` statement that exports the component and it is available to other components by using import. There can be only one default export per file, but there can be multiple named exports:

```js
import React, { Component } from 'react';
import logo from './logo.svg';
import './App.css';

class App extends Component {
  render() {
    return (
      <div className="App">
        <header className="App-header">
          <img src={logo} className="App-logo" alt="logo" />
          <h1 className="App-title">Welcome to React</h1>
```

```
      </header>
      <p className="App-intro">
        To get started, edit <code>src/App.js</code> and save to reload.
      </p>
    </div>
  );
  }
}
```

```
export default App;
```

The following example shows how to import default and named exports:

```
import React from 'react' // Import default value
import { Component } from 'react' // Import named value
```

And the exports looks like the following:

```
export default React // Default export
export {Component} // Named export
```

Basics of ES6

ES6 (ECMAScript 2015) was released in 2015 and it introduced a lot of new features. ECMAScript is a standardized scripting language and JavaScript is one implementation of it. Here, we will go through the most important features released in ES6 that we are going to use in the next sections.

Understanding constants

Constants, or immutable variables, can be defined by using a `const` keyword. When using the `const` keyword, the variable content cannot be reassigned:

```
const PI = 3.14159;
```

The scope of `const` is block-scoped, which is the same as `let` have. It means that the `const` variable can be used only inside the block where it is defined. In practice, the block is the area between curly brackets { }. The following sample code shows how the scope works. The second `console.log` statement gives an error because we are trying to use the `total` variable outside the scope:

```
var count = 10;
if(count > 5) {
```

```
    const total = count * 2;
    console.log(total); // Prints 20 to console
}
console.log(total); // Error, outside the scope
```

It is good to know that if the const is an object or array, the content can be changed. The following example demonstrates that:

```
const myObj = {foo : 3};
myObj.foo = 5; // This is ok
```

Arrow functions

Arrow functions make function declaration much more compact. The traditional way of defining a function in JavaScript is using a function keyword. The following function gets one argument and just returns the argument value:

```
function hello(greeting) {
    return greeting;
}
```

By using the ES6 arrow function, the function looks as follows:

```
const hello = greeting => { greeting }

// function call
hello('Hello World'); // returns Hello World
```

If you have more than one argument, you have to wrap the arguments in parentheses and separate arguments with a comma. The following function gets two parameters and returns the sum of the parameters. If the function body is an expression, you don't need to use the return keyword. The expression is always implicitly returned from the function:

```
const calcSum = (x, y) => { x + y }

// function call
calcSum(2, 3); // returns 5
```

If the function doesn't have any arguments, the syntax is the following:

```
() => { ... }
```

Template literals

Template literals can be used to concatenate strings. The traditional way to concatenate strings is to use the plus operator:

```
var person = {firstName: 'John', lastName: 'Johnson'};
var greeting = "Hello " + ${person.firstName} + " " + ${person.lastName};
```

With the template literals, the syntax is the following. You have to use backticks (` `) instead of single or double quotes:

```
var person = {firstName: 'John', lastName: 'Johnson'};
var greeting = `Hello ${person.firstName} ${person.lastName}`;
```

Classes and inheritance

Class definition in ES6 is similar to other object oriented languages like Java or C#. The keyword for defining the classes is `class`. The class can have fields, constructors, and class methods. The following sample code shows the ES6 class:

```
class Person {
    constructor(firstName, lastName) {
        this.firstName = firstName;
        this.lastName = lastName;
    }
}
```

Inheritance is done with an `extends` keyword. The following sample code shows an `Employee` class that inherits a `Person` class. Therefore, it inherits all fields from the parent class and can have its own fields that are specific to the employee. In the constructor, we first call the parent class constructor by using the `super` keyword. That call is required and you will get an error if it is missing:

```
class Employee extends Person {
    constructor(firstName, lastName, title, salary) {
        super(firstName, lastName);
        this.title= title;
        this.salary = salary;
    }
}
```

Although ES6 is already quite old but it is still only partially supported by modern web browsers. Babel is a JavaScript compiler that is used to compile ES6 to an older version that is compatible with all browsers. You can test the compiler on the Babel website (`https://babeljs.io`). The following screenshot shows the arrow function compilating back to the older JavaScript syntax:

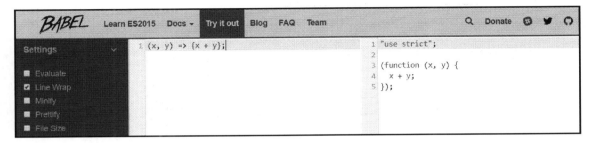

JSX and styling

JSX is the syntax extension for JavaScript. It is not mandatory to use JSX with React but there are some benefits that make development easier. JSX, for example, prevents injection attacks because all values are escaped in the JSX before they are rendered. The most useful feature is that you can embed JavaScript expressions in the JSX by wrapping it with curly brackets and that will be used a lot in the following chapters. In this example, we can access the component props when using JSX. The component props are covered in the next section:

```
class Hello extends React.Component {
  render() {
    return <h1>Hello World {this.props.user}</h1>;
  }
}
```

You can also pass a JavaScript expression as props:

```
<Hello count={2+2} />
```

JSX is compiled to the `React.createElement()` calls by Babel. You can use both internal or external styling with the React JSX elements. The following are two examples of inline styling. The first one defines the style straight inside the `div` element:

```
<div style={{height: 20, width: 200}}>
  Hello
</div>
```

And the second example creates the style object first, which is then used in the `div` element. The object name should use the camelCase naming convention:

```
const divStyle = {
  color: 'red',
  height: 30
};

const MyComponent = () => (
  <div style={divStyle}>Hello</div>
);
```

As shown in the previous section, you can import a style sheet to the React component. To reference classes from the external CSS file, you should use a `className` attribute:

```
import './App.js';

...

<div className="App-header">
  This is my app
</div>
```

Props and state

Props and state are the input data for rendering the component. Both props and state are actually JavaScript objects, and the component is re-rendered when props or state are changing.

The props are immutable, so the component cannot change its props. The props are received from the parent component. The component can access the props through the `this.props` object. For example, take a look at the following component:

```
class Hello extends React.Component {
  render() {
    return <h1>Hello World {this.props.user}</h1>;
  }
}
```

The parent component can send props to the `Hello` component in the following way:

```
<Hello user="John" />
```

When the `Hello` component is rendered, it shows the `Hello World John` text.

The state can be changed inside the component. The initial value of the state is given in the component's constructor. The state can be accessed by using the `this.state` object. The scope of the state is the component, so it cannot be used outside the component where it is defined. As you can see in the following example, the props are passed to the constructor as an argument and the state is initialized in the constructor. The value of the state can then be rendered in JSX using curly brackets, `{this.state.user}`:

```
class Hello extends React.Component {
  constructor(props) {
    super(props);
    this.state = {user: 'John'}
  }

  render() {
    return <h1>Hello World {this.state.user}</h1>;
  }
}
```

The state can contain multiple values of different types because it is a JavaScript object, as in the following example:

```
constructor(props) {
  super(props);
  this.state = {firstName: 'John', lastName: 'Johnson', age: 30}
}
```

The value of the state is changed using the `setState` method:

```
this.setState({firstName: 'Jim', age: 31});  // Change state value
```

You should never update the state by using the equals operator because then the React doesn't re-render the component. The only way to change state is to use the `setState` method, which triggers re-rendering:

```
this.state.firstName = 'Jim'; // WRONG
```

The `setState` method is asynchronous and therefore you cannot be sure when the state will be updated. The `setState` method has a callback function that is executed when the state has been updated.

The usage of the state is always optional and it increases the complexity of the component. The components that have only the props are called **stateless** components. It will always render the same output when having the same input, which means they are really easy to test. The components that have both state and props are called **stateful** components. The following is an example of the simple stateless component and it is defined using the class. You can also define it by using the function:

```
export default class MyTitle extends Component {
  render() {
    return (
      <div>
        <h1>{this.props.text}</h1>
      </div>
    );
  };
};


// The MyTitle component can be then used in other component and text value
is passed to props
<MyTitle text="Hello" />
// Or you can use other component's state
<MyTitle text={this.state.username} />
```

If you are updating the state values that depend on the current state, you should pass an update function to the setState() method instead of the object. A common case to demonstrate this situation is the counter example shown here:

```
// This solution might not work correctly
incerementCounter = () => {
 this.setState({count: this.state.count + 1});
}

// The correct way is the following
incrementCounter = () => {
  this.setState((prevState) => {
    return {count: prevState.count + 1}
  });
}
```

Component life cycle methods

The React component has many life cycle methods that you can override. These methods are executed at certain phases of the component's life cycle. The names of the life cycle methods are logical and you can almost guess when they are going to be executed. The life cycle methods that have a prefix are executed before anything happens and the methods with a prefix are executed after something happens. Mounting is one phase of the component life cycle and it is the moment when the component is created and inserted into the DOM. Two life cycle methods that we have already covered are executed when the component mounts: `constructor()` and `render()`.

A useful method in the mounting phase is `componentDidMount()`, which is called after the component has been mounted. This method is suitable for calling some REST APIs to get data, for example. The following sample code gives an example of using the `componentDidMount()` method.

In the following example code, we first set the initial value of `this.state.user` to John. Then, when the component is mounted, we change the value to `Jim`:

```
class Hello extends React.Component {
  constructor(props) {
    super(props);
    this.state = {user: 'John'}
  }

  componentDidMount() {
    this.setState({user: 'Jim'});
  }

  render() {
    return <h1>Hello World {this.state.user}</h1>;
  }
}
```

There is also a `componentWillMount()` life cycle method that is called before the component is mounted, but Facebook recommends not to use that because it might be used for internal development purposes.

A `shouldComponentUpdate()` method is called when the state or props have been updated and before the component is rendered. The method gets new props as the first argument and a new state as the second argument, and it returns the Boolean value. If the returned value is `true`, the component will be re-rendered; otherwise, it won't be re-rendered. This method allows you to avoid useless renders and improves performance:

```
shouldComponentUpdate(nextProps, nextState) {
  // This function should return a boolean, whether the component should
  re-render.
  return true;
}
```

A `componentWillUnmount()` life cycle method is called before the component is removed from the DOM. This is a good point to clean resources, clear timers, or cancel requests.

Error boundaries are the components that catch JavaScript errors in their child component tree. They should also log these errors and show fallback in the user interface. For that, there is a life cycle method called `componentDidCatch()`. It works with the React components like the standard JavaScript `catch` block.

Handling lists with React

For list-handling, we introduce a new JavaScript method, `map()`, which is handy when you have to manipulate a list. The `map()` method creates a new array with the results of calling a function to each element in the original array. In the following example, each array element is multiplied by two:

```
const arr = [1, 2, 3, 4];

const resArr = arr.map(x => x * 2); // resArr = [2, 4, 6, 8]
```

The `map()` method also has the `index` second argument, which is useful when handling lists in React. The list items in React need a unique key that is used to detect rows that have been changed, added, or deleted.

The following example shows components that transform the array of integers to the array of list items and render these in the `ul` element:

```
class App extends React.Component {
  render() {
    const data = [1, 2, 3, 4, 5];
    const rows = data.map((number, index) =>
      <li key={index}>Listitem {number}</li>
```

```
    );

    return (
     <div>
      <ul>{rows}</ul>
     </div>
    );
   }
  }
```

The following screenshot shows what the component looks like when it is rendered:

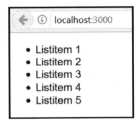

If the data is an array of objects, it would be nicer to present the data in table format. The idea is the same as with the list, but now we just map the array to table rows and render these in the table element, as shown in the following code:

```
class App extends Component {
  render() {
    const data = [{brand: 'Ford', model: 'Mustang'},
    {brand:'VW', model: 'Beetle'}, {brand: 'Tesla', model: 'Model S'}];
    const tableRows = data.map((item, index) =>
     <tr key={index}><td>{item.brand}</td><td>{item.model}</td></tr>
    );

    return (
     <div>
      <table><tbody>{tableRows}</tbody></table>
     </div>
    );
   }
  }
```

The following screenshot shows what the component looks like when it is rendered:

Handling events with React

Event handling in React is similar to handling DOM element events. The difference, compared to HTML event handling, is that event naming uses camelCase in React. The following sample code adds an event listener to the button and shows an alert message when the button is pressed:

```
class App extends React.Component {
  // This is called when the button is pressed
  buttonPressed = () => {
    alert('Button pressed');
  }
  render() {
    return (
      <div>
        <button onClick={this.buttonPressed}>Press Me</button>
      </div>
    );
  }
}
```

In React, you cannot return `false` from the event handler to prevent default behavior. Instead, you should call the `preventDefault()` method. In the following example, we are using a form and we want to prevent form submission:

```
class MyForm extends React.Component {
  // This is called when the form is submitted
  handleSubmit(event) {
    alert('Form submit');
    event.preventDefault();  // Prevents default behavior
  }

  render() {
    return (
      <form onSubmit={this.handleSubmit}>
```

```
        <input type="submit" value="Submit" />
      </form>
    );
  }
}
```

Handling forms with React

Form handling is a little bit different with React. An HTML form will navigate to the next page when it is submitted. A common case is that we want to invoke a JavaScript function that has access to form data after submission and avoid navigating to the next page. We already covered how to avoid submit in the previous section using `preventDefault()`.

Let's first create a minimalistic form with one input field and the submit button. To be able to get the value of the input field, we are using the `onChange` event handler. When the value of the input field is changed, the new value will be saved to state. The `this.setState({text: event.target.value});` statement gets the value from the input field and saves it to the state called `text`. Finally, we will show the typed value when a user presses the submit button. The following is the source code for our first form:

```
class App extends Component {
  constructor(props) {
    super(props);
    this.state = {text: ''};
  }

  // Save input box value to state when it has been changed
  inputChanged = (event) => {
    this.setState({text: event.target.value});
  }

  handleSubmit = (event) => {
    alert(`You typed: ${this.state.text}`);
    event.preventDefault();
  }

  render() {
    return (
      <form onSubmit={this.handleSubmit}>
        <input type="text" onChange={this.inputChanged}
            value={this.state.text}/>
        <input type="submit" value="Press me"/>
      </form>
    );
```

```
    }
  }
```

The following is a screenshot of our form component after the **Submit** button has been pressed:

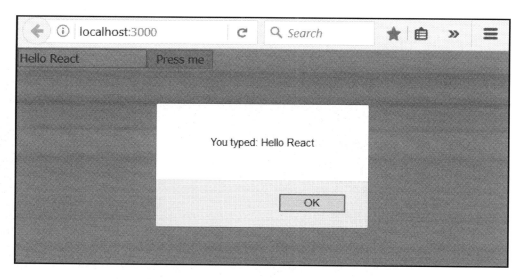

Now is a good time to look at the React Developer Tools, which are handy tools for debugging React apps. If we open the React Developer Tools with our React form app and type something into the input field, we can see how the value of the state changes. We can inspect the current value of both props and state. The following screenshot shows how the state changes when we type something into the input field:

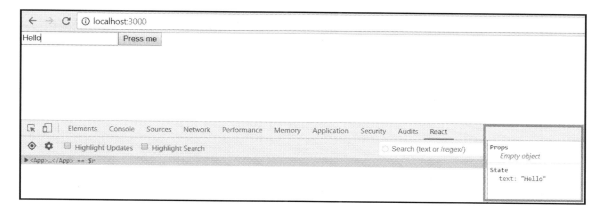

Typically, we have more than one input field in the form. One way to handle multiple input fields is to add as many change handlers as we have input fields. But this creates a lot of boilerplate code, which we want to avoid. Therefore, we add the name attributes to our input fields and we can utilize that in the change handler to identify which input field triggers the change handler. The name attribute value of the input field must be the same as the name of the state where we want to save the value.

The handler now looks like the following. If the input field that triggers the handler is the first name field, then `event.target.name` is `firstName` and the typed value will be saved to a state called `firstName`. In this way, we can handle all input fields with the one change handler:

```
inputChanged = (event) => {
    this.setState({[event.target.name]: event.target.value});
}
```

The following is the full source code of the component:

```
class App extends Component {
  constructor(props) {
    super(props);
    this.state = {firstName: '', lastName: '', email: ''};
  }

  inputChanged = (event) => {
    this.setState({[event.target.name]: event.target.value});
  }

  handleSubmit = (event) => {
    alert(`Hello ${this.state.firstName} ${this.state.lastName}`);
    event.preventDefault();
  }

  render() {
    return (
      <form onSubmit={this.handleSubmit}>
        <label>First name </label>
        <input type="text" name="firstName" onChange={this.inputChanged}
            value={this.state.firstName}/><br/>
        <label>Last name </label>
        <input type="text" name="lastName" onChange={this.inputChanged}
            value={this.state.lastName}/><br/>
        <label>Email </label>
        <input type="email" name="email" onChange={this.inputChanged}
            value={this.state.email}/><br/>
        <input type="submit" value="Press me"/>
```

```
        </form>
      );
    }
  }
```

The following is a screenshot of our form component after the **Submit** button has been pressed:

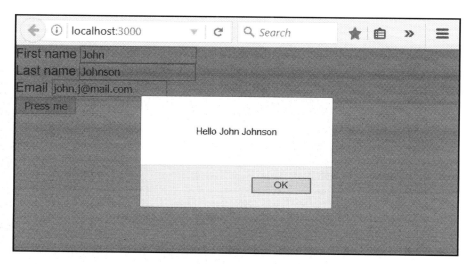

Summary

In this chapter, we started to discover React, which we are going to use to build our frontend. Before starting to develop with React, we covered the basics, such as the React component, JSX, props, and state. In our frontend development, we are using ES6, which makes our code cleaner. We went through the features that we need for further development. We also learned how to handle forms and events with React.

Questions

1. What is the React component?
2. What are state and props?
3. How does data flow in the React app?
4. What is the difference between stateless and stateful components?
5. What is JSX?
6. What are component life cycle methods?
7. How should we handle events in React?
8. How should we handle forms in React?

Further reading

Packt has other great resources for learning about React:

- `https://www.packtpub.com/web-development/getting-started-react`
- `https://www.packtpub.com/web-development/react-16-essentials-second-edition`

Consuming the REST API with React

7

This chapter explains networking with React. We will learn about promises, which make asynchronous code cleaner and more readable. For networking, we will use the `fetch` library. As an example, we use the GitHub REST API to demonstrate how to consume RESTful Web Services with React.

In this chapter, we will look at the following:

- Using promises
- How to use Fetch
- How to make requests to the REST API
- How to handle responses from the REST API
- How to create a React app that consumes the REST API

Technical requirements

In this book, we are using the Windows operating system, but all tools are available for Linux and macOS as Node.js and `create-react-app` have to be installed.

Using promises

The traditional way to handle an asynchronous operation is to use callback functions for the success or failure of the operation. One of the callback functions is called, depending on the result of the call. The following example shows the idea of using the callback function:

```
function doAsyncCall(success, failure) {
    // Do some api call
```

```
        if (SUCCEED)
            success(resp);
        else
            failure(err);
    }

    success(response) {
        // Do something with response
    }

    failure(error) {
        // Handle error
    }

    doAsyncCall(success, failure);
```

A promise is an object that represents the result of an asynchronous operation. The use of promises simplifies the code when doing asynchronous calls. Promises are non-blocking.

A promise can be in one of three states:

- **Pending**: Initial state
- **Fulfilled**: Successful operation
- **Rejected**: Failed operation

With promises, we can do asynchronous calls if the API we are using supports promises. In the next example, the asynchronous call is done and, when the response is returned, the function inside then is executed and it takes the response as an argument:

```
doAsyncCall()
.then(response => // Do something with the response);
```

You can chain thens together, which means that you can run multiple asynchronous operations one after another:

```
doAsyncCall()
.then(response => // Get some result from the response)
.then(result => // Do something with the result);
```

You can also add error-handling to promises by using catch():

```
doAsyncCall()
.then(response => // Get some result from the response)
.then(result => // Do something with result);
.catch(error => console.error(error))
```

There is a more modern way to handle asynchronous calls, with async/await, which was introduced in ECMAScript 2017. It is yet not as widely supported by browsers as promises. async/await is actually based on the promises. To use async/await, you have to define an async function that can contain await expressions. The following is an example of an asynchronous call with async/await. As you can see, you can write the code in a similar way to synchronous code:

```
doAsyncCall = async () => {
    const response = await fetch('http://someapi.com');
    const result = await response.json();
    // Do something with the result
}
```

For error-handling, you can use try...catch with async/await, as shown in the following example:

```
doAsyncCall = async () => {
  try {
    const response = await fetch('http://someapi.com');
    const result = await response.json();
    // Do something with the result
  }
  catch(err) {
    console.error(err);
  }
}
```

Using the Fetch API

With the Fetch API, you can make web requests. The idea of the Fetch API is similar to traditional XMLHttpRequest, but the Fetch API also supports promises that makes it more straightforward to use.

The Fetch API provides a fetch() method that has one mandatory argument, which is the path of the resource you are calling. In the case of a web request, it will be the URL of the service. For a simple GET method call, which returns a JSON response, the syntax is the following. The fetch() method returns a promise that contains the response. You can use the json() method to parse the JSON body from the response:

```
fetch('http://someapi.com')
.then(response => response.json())
.then(result => console.log(result));
.catch(error => console.error(error))
```

To use another HTTP method, such as POST, you can define it in the second argument of the `fetch` method. The second argument is the object where you can define multiple request settings. The following source code makes the request using the POST method:

```
fetch('http://someapi.com', {method: 'POST'})
.then(response => response.json())
.then(result => console.log(result))
.catch(error => console.error(error));
```

You can also add headers inside the second argument. The following `fetch` call contains the `'Content-Type' : 'application/json'` header:

```
fetch('http://someapi.com',
 {
  method: 'POST',
  headers:{'Content-Type': 'application/json'}
 }
.then(response => response.json())
.then(result => console.log(result))
.catch(error => console.error(error));
```

If you have to send JSON-encoded data inside the request body, the syntax is the following:

```
fetch('http://someapi.com',
 {
  method: 'POST',
  headers:{'Content-Type': 'application/json'},
  body: JSON.stringify(data)
 }
.then(response => response.json())
.then(result => console.log(result))
.catch(error => console.error(error));
```

You can also use other libraries for the network calls. One very popular library is `axios` (`https://github.com/axios/axios`), which you can install to your React app with npm. `axios` has some benefits, such as automatic transform for JSON data. The following code shows the example call with `axios`:

```
axios.get('http://someapi.com')
.then(response => console.log(response))
.catch(error => console.log(error));
```

`axios` has its own call methods for the different HTTP methods. For example, if you want to make a DELETE request, `axios` provides the `axios.delete` method.

Practical examples

We will go through two examples of using some open REST APIs. First, we will make a React app that shows the current weather in London. The weather is fetched from **OpenWeatherMap** (https://openweathermap.org/). You need to register to OpenWeatherMap to get an API key. We will use a free account as that is enough for our needs. When you have registered, navigate to your account info to find the API keys tab. There you'll see the API key that you need for your React weather app:

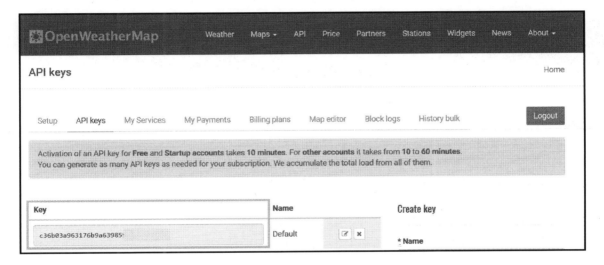

Let's create a new React app with `create-react-app`. Open the PowerShell or other terminal you are using, and type the following command:

```
create-react-app weatherapp
```

Move to the `weatherApp` folder:

```
cd weatherapp
```

Start your app with the following command:

```
npm start
```

Open your project folder with the VS Code and open the App.js file in the editor view. Remove all code inside the `<div className="App"></div>` divider. Now your source code should look like the following:

```
import React, { Component } from 'react';
import './App.css';

class App extends Component {
  render() {
    return (
      <div className="App">
      </div>
    );
  }
}

export default App;
```

If you have installed *Reactjs code snippets* to VS Code, you can create a default constructor automatically by typing `con`. There are lots of different shortcuts for typical React methods, such as `cdm` for `componentDidMount()`.

First, we add a necessary constructor and state. We will show the temperature, description, and weather icon in our app, therefore, we define three state values. We will also add one Boolean state to indicate the status of fetch loading. The following is the source code of the constructor:

```
constructor(props) {
  super(props);
  this.state = {temp: 0, desc: '', icon: '', loading: true}
}
```

When you are using a REST API, you should first inspect the response to be able to get values from the JSON data. In the following example, you can see the address that returns the current weather for London. Copy the address to a browser and you can see the JSON response data:

```
api.openweathermap.org/data/2.5/weather?q=London&units=Metric&APIkey=YOUR_K
EY
```

From the response, you can see that the `temp` can be accessed using `main.temp`. The `description` and `icon` are inside the `weather` array, which has only one element and we can access it using `weather[0].description` and `weather[0].icon`:

The REST API call is done with the `fetch` in the `componentDidMount()` life cycle method. After the successful response, we save the weather data to the state and change the `loading` state to `false`. After the state has been changed, the component will be re-rendered. We will implement the `render()` method in the next step. The following is the source code of the `componentDidMount()` method:

```
componentDidMount() {
  fetch('http://api.openweathermap.org/data/2.5/weather?
    q=London&units=Metric
    &APIkey=c36b03a963176b9a639859e6cf279299')
  .then(response => response.json())
  .then(responseData => {
    this.setState({
      temp: responseData.main.temp,
      desc: responseData.weather[0].description,
      icon: responseData.weather[0].icon,
      loading: false
    })
  })
  .catch(err => console.error(err));
}
```

After you have added the `componentDidMount()` method, the request is done when the component is mounted. We can check that everything is done correctly using the React Developer Tool. Open your app in a browser and open your browser developer tool's **React** tab. Now you can see that the state is updated with the values from the response. You can also check from the **Network** tab that the request status is 200 OK:

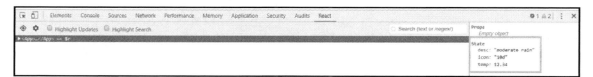

Finally, we implement the `render()` method to show weather values. We are using conditional rendering, otherwise, we get an error because we don't have image code in the first render call and image upload won't succeed. To show the weather icon, we have to add `http://openweathermap.org/img/w/` before the icon code and `.png` after the icon code. Then, we can set the concatenated image URL to the `img` element's `src` attribute. The temperature and description are shown in the paragraph element. The °C HTML entity shows the Celsius degrees symbol:

```
render() {
  const imgSrc =
`http://openweathermap.org/img/w/${this.state.icon}.png`;

  if (this.state.loading) {
    return <p>Loading</p>;
  }
  else {
    return (
      <div className="App">
        <p>Temperature: {this.state.temp} °C</p>
        <p>Description: {this.state.desc}</p>
        <img src={imgSrc} alt="Weather icon" />
      </div>
    );
  }
}
```

Now your app should be ready. When you open it in a browser, it should look like the following image:

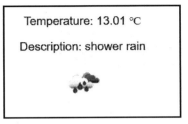

The source code of the whole `App.js` file looks as follows:

```javascript
import React, { Component } from 'react';
import './App.css';

class App extends Component {
  constructor(props) {
    super(props);
    this.state = {temp: 0, desc: '', icon: ''}
  }

  componentDidMount() {
    fetch('http://api.openweathermap.org/data/2.5/weather?
      q=London&units=Metric&APIkey=YOUR_KEY')
    .then(response => response.json())
    .then(responseData => {
      this.setState({
         temp: responseData.main.temp,
        desc: responseData.weather[0].description,
        icon: responseData.weather[0].icon
      });
    });
  }
  render() {
    const imgSrc = 'http://openweathermap.org/img/w/' +
    this.state.icon + '.png';
```

```
      return (
        <div className="App">
          <p>Temperature: {this.state.temp}</p>
          <p>Description: {this.state.desc}</p>
          <img src={imgSrc} />
        </div>
      );
    }
}

export default App;
```

In this second example, we are going to use the GitHub API to fetch repositories by a keyword. With the same steps as in the previous example, create a new React app called `restgithub`. Start the app and open the project folder with the VS Code.

Remove the extra code inside the `<div className="App"></div>` divider from the `App.js` file and again your `App.js` code should look like the following sample code:

```
import React, { Component } from 'react';
import './App.css';

class App extends Component {
  render() {
    return (
      <div className="App">
      </div>
    );
  }
}

export default App;
```

The URL of the GitHub REST API is the following:

```
https://api.github.com/search/repositories?q=KEYWORD
```

Let's inspect the JSON response by typing the URL into a browser and using the `react` keyword. From the response, we see that repositories are returned as a JSON array called `items`. From the individual repositories, we will show the `full_name` and `html_url` values. We will present the data in the table and use the `map` function to transform the values to table rows, as shown in the previous chapter:

We are going to make the REST API call with the keyword from the user input. Therefore, we can't make the REST API call in the `componentDidMount()` method because, in that phase, we don't have the user input available. One way to implement this is to create an input field and button. The user types the keyword into the input field and the REST API call is done when the button is pressed. We need two states, one for the user input and one for the data from the JSON response. The following is the source code of the `constructor`. The type of data state is an array because repositories are returned as JSON arrays in the response:

```
constructor(props) {
  super(props);
  this.state = { keyword: '', data: [] };
}
```

Next, we implement the input field and the button into the `render()` method. We also have to add a change listener to our input field to be able to save the input value to the state, called `keyword`. The button has a click listener that invokes the function that will do the REST API call with the given keyword:

```
fetchData = () => {
  // REST API call comes here
}
handleChange = (e) => {
  this.setState({keyword: e.target.value});
}

render() {
  return (
    <div className="App">
      <input type="text" onChange={this.handleChange} />
      <button onClick={this.fetchData} value={this.state.keyword}
>Fetch</button>
    </div>
  );
}
```

In the `fetchData` function, we concatenate the `url` and `keyword` state by using template literals. Then we save the `items` array from the response to the state, called `data`. The following is the source code of the `fetchData` function:

```
fetchData = () => {
  const url = `https://api.github.com/search/repositories?
    q=${this.state.keyword}`;
  fetch(url)
  .then(response => response.json())
  .then(responseData => {
    this.setState({data : responseData.items });
  });
}
```

In the `render` method, we first use the `map` function to transform the `data` state to table rows. The `url` repository will be the `href` of the link element:

```
render() {
  const tableRows = this.state.data.map((item, index) =>
    <tr key={index}><td>{item.full_name}</td>
    <td><a href={item.html_url}>{item.html_url}</a></td></tr>);

  return (
    <div className="App">
```

```
        <input type="text" onChange={this.handleChange} />
        <button onClick={this.fetchData} value={this.state.keyword}
>Fetch</button>
        <table><tbody>{tableRows}</tbody></table>
      </div>
    );
```

The following screenshot shows the final app when using the React keyword in the REST API call:

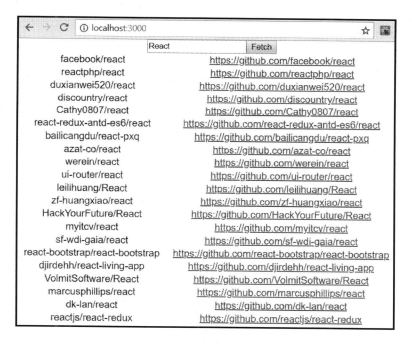

The source code of the whole `App.js` file looks like the following:

```
import React, { Component } from 'react';
import './App.css';

class App extends Component {
  constructor(props) {
    super(props);
    this.state = { keyword: '', data: [] };
  }

  fetchData = () => {
    const url = `https://api.github.com/search/repositories?
      q=${this.state.keyword}`;
```

```
      fetch(url)
      .then(response => response.json())
      .then(responseData => {
        this.setState({data : responseData.items });
      });
    }
    handleChange = (e) => {
      this.setState({keyword: e.target.value});
    }

    render() {
      const tableRows = this.state.data.map((item, index) =>
        <tr key={index}><td>{item.full_name}</td>
        <td><a href={item.html_url}>{item.html_url}</a></td></tr>);

      return (
        <div className="App">
          <input type="text" onChange={this.handleChange} />
          <button onClick={this.fetchData}
          value={this.state.keyword} >Fetch</button>
          <table><tbody>{tableRows}</tbody></table>
        </div>
      );
    }
  }
```

Summary

In this chapter, we focused on networking with React. We started with promises that make asynchronous network calls easier to implement. It is a cleaner way to handle calls, and much better than using traditional callback functions. In this book, we are using the Fetch API for networking, therefore we went through the basics of using fetch. We implemented two practical React apps that calling open REST APIs and we presented the response data in the browser. In the next chapter we will look some useful React component that we are going to use in our frontend.

Questions

1. What is a promise?
2. What is `fetch`?
3. How should you call the REST API from the React app?
4. How should you handle the response of the REST API call?

Further reading

Packt has other great resources for learning about React:

- https://www.packtpub.com/web-development/getting-started-react
- https://www.packtpub.com/web-development/react-16-essentials-second-edition

8
Useful Third-Party Components for React

React is component-based and we can find a lot of useful third-party components that we can use in our apps. In this chapter, we are going to look at several components that we are going to use in our frontend. We will see how to find suitable components and how you can use these in your own apps.

In this chapter, we will look at the following:

- How to find third-party React components
- How to install components
- How to use the React Table component
- How to use the modal window component
- How to use the Material UI component library
- How to manage routing in React

Technical requirements

In this book, we are using the Windows operating system but all tools are available for Linux and macOS as Node.js and `create-react-app` have to be installed.

Using third-party React components

There are a lot of nice React components available for different purposes. Our first task is to find a suitable component for your needs. One good site for searching components is JS.coach (`https://js.coach/`). You just have to type in a keyword, search, and select React from the list of frameworks. In the following screenshot, you can see the search of the table components for React:

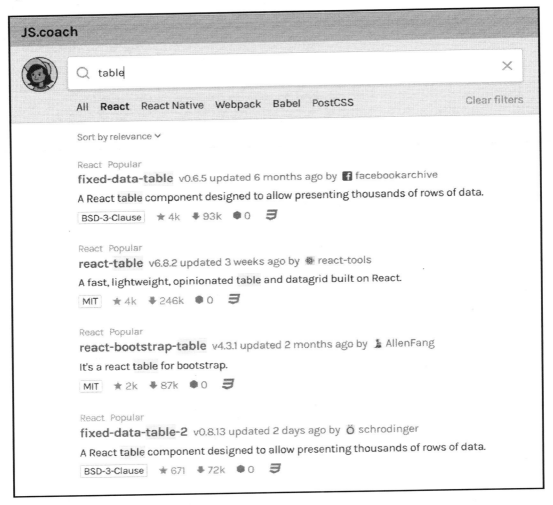

Another good source for React components is Awesome React Components (`https://github.com/brillout/awesome-react-components`).

Components often have good documentation that helps you to utilize them in your own React app. Let's see how we can install a third-party component to our app and start to use it. Navigate to the JS.coach site, type `list` to search the input field, and filter by **React**. From the search results, you can find the list component, called `react-tiny-virtual-list`:

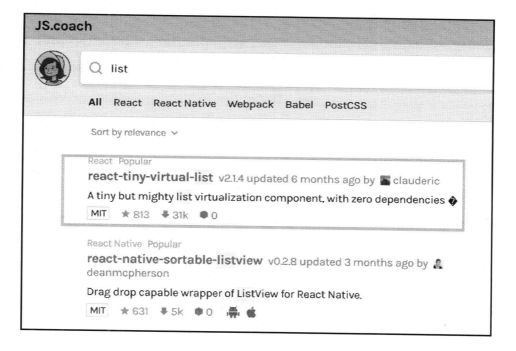

Click the component link to see more detailed info about the component. Quite often, you can find the installation instructions there and also some simple examples of how to use the component. The info page often provides the address of a component's website or GitHub repository, where you can find the full documentation:

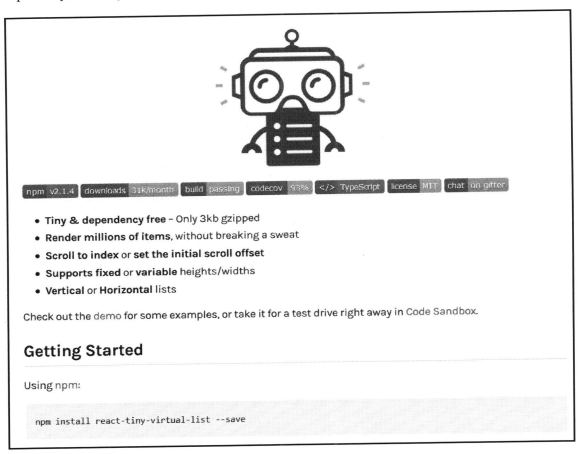

- **Tiny & dependency free** – Only 3kb gzipped
- **Render millions of items**, without breaking a sweat
- **Scroll to index** or **set the initial scroll offset**
- **Supports fixed** or **variable** heights/widths
- **Vertical** or **Horizontal** lists

Check out the demo for some examples, or take it for a test drive right away in Code Sandbox.

Getting Started

Using npm:

```
npm install react-tiny-virtual-list --save
```

As you can see from the component's info page, the installation of the components is done using npm. The syntax of the command is as follows:

```
npm install component_name --save
```

Or, if you are using Yarn, it is as follows:

```
yarn add component_name
```

The `--save` parameter saves the component's dependency to the `package.json` file that is in the root folder of your React app. If you are using npm version 5 or greater, this is done by default, without the `--save` parameter. With Yarn, you don't have to specify that because it saves the component dependency by default.

Now we install the `react-tiny-virtual-list` component to the `myapp` React app that we created in the previous chapter. You have to move to your app root folder and type the following command:

```
npm install react-tiny-virtual-list --save
```

If you open the `package.json` file from your app root folder, you can see that the component is now added to the dependencies:

```
{
  "name": "myapp",
  "version": "0.1.0",
  "private": true,
  "dependencies": {
    "react": "^16.3.2",
    "react-dom": "^16.3.2",
    "react-scripts": "1.1.4",
    "react-tiny-virtual-list": "^2.1.4"
  },
  "scripts": {
    "start": "react-scripts start",
    "build": "react-scripts build",
    "test": "react-scripts test --env=jsdom",
    "eject": "react-scripts eject"
  }
}
```

Installed components are saved to the node_modules folder in your app. If you open that folder, you should find the react-tiny-virtual-list folder:

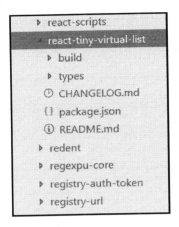

Now, if you push your React app source code to GitHub, you should not include node_modules because that folder is really big. The create-react-app contains .gitignore file that excludes node_modules folder from the repository. The content of the .gitignore file looks following:

```
# See https://help.github.com/ignore-files/ for more about ignoring files.

# dependencies
/node_modules

# testing
/coverage

# production
/build

# misc
.DS_Store
.env.local
.env.development.local
.env.test.local
.env.production.local

npm-debug.log*
yarn-debug.log*
yarn-error.log*
```

The idea is that when you clone your app from the GitHub, you type the `npm install` command, that reads dependencies from the `package.json` file and downloads these to your app.

The final step to start using your installed component is to import it into the files where you are using it:

```
import VirtualList from 'react-tiny-virtual-list';
```

React Table

React Table (`https://react-table.js.org`) is a flexible table component for React apps. It has many useful features, such as filtering, sorting, and pivoting. Let's use the GitHub REST API app that we created in the previous chapter:

1. Install the `react-table` component. Open PowerShell and move to the `restgithub` folder, which is the root folder of the app. Install the component by typing the following command:

   npm install react-table --save

2. Open the `App.js` file with the VS Code and remove all code inside the `render()` method except the `return` statement with the divider containing the button and input field. Now the `App.js` file should look like the following:

   ```
   import React, { Component } from 'react';
   import './App.css';

   class App extends Component {
     constructor(props) {
       super(props);
       this.state = { keyword: '', data: [] };
     }

     fetchData = () => {
       const url = `https://api.github.com/search/repositories?
       q=${this.state.keyword}`;
       fetch(url)
   ```

```
      .then(response => response.json())
      .then(responseData => {
        this.setState({data : responseData.items });
      });
  }
  handleChange = (e) => {
    this.setState({keyword: e.target.value});
  }

  render() {
    return (
      <div className="App">
        <input type="text" onChange={this.handleChange} />
        <button onClick={this.fetchData} value=
          {this.state.keyword} >Fetch</button>
      </div>
    );
  }
}

export default App;
```

3. Import the `react-table` component and style sheet by adding the following lines at the beginning of the `App.js` file:

```
import ReactTable from "react-table";
import 'react-table/react-table.css';
```

4. To fill React Table with data, you have to pass the data prop to the component. Data can be an array or object and therefore we can use our state, called `data`. Columns are defined using the columns prop and that prop is required:

```
<ReactTable
  data={data}
  columns={columns}
/>
```

5. We will define our columns by creating the array of column objects into the `render()` method. In a column object, you have to define at least the header of the column and the data accessor. The data accessor values come from our REST API response data. You can see that our response data contains an object called `owner`, and we can show these values using the `owner.field_name` syntax:

```
const columns = [{
    Header: 'Name',  // Header of the column
```

```
      accessor: 'full_name' // Value accessor
    }, {
     Header: 'URL',
     accessor: 'html_url',
    }, {
     Header: 'Owner',
     accessor: 'owner.login',
  }]
```

6. Add the React Table component to our `render()` method, and then the source code of the method looks like the following:

```
render() {
  const columns = [{
    Header: 'Name', // Header of the column
    accessor: 'full_name' // Value accessor
  }, {
    Header: 'URL',
    accessor: 'html_url',
  }, {
    Header: 'Owner',
    accessor: 'owner.login',
  }]

  return (
    <div className="App">
      <input type="text" onChange={this.handleChange} />
      <button onClick={this.fetchData}
       value={this.state.keyword} >Fetch</button>
      <ReactTable
        data={this.state.data}
        columns={columns}
      />
    </div>
  );
}
```

7. Run the app and navigate to `localhost:3000`. The table looks quite nice. It has sorting and paging available by default:

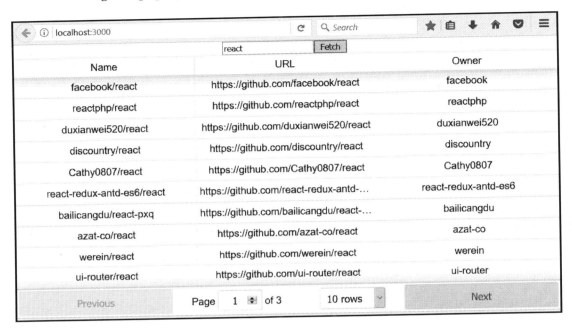

Filtering is disabled by default but you can enable it using the `filterable` prop in the `ReactTable` component. You can also set the page size of the table:

```
<ReactTable
    data={this.state.data}
    columns={columns}
    filterable={true}
    defaultPageSize = {10}
/>
```

Now you should see the filter element in your table. You can filter using any column, but there is also an option to set the filtering and sorting in the column level:

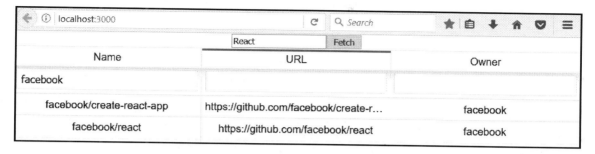

You can find different props for the table and columns from the React Table website.

Cell renderers can be used to customize the content of the table cell. The following example shows how you can render a button to a table cell. The function in the cell renderer passes value as the argument and, in this case, the value will be full_name, which is defined in the accessor of the column. The other option is to pass a row, which passes the whole row object to the function. Then you have to define the btnClick function, which is invoked when the button is pressed and you can do something with the value that is sent to the function:

```
render() {
  const columns = [{
    Header: 'Name', // Header of the column
    accessor: 'full_name' // Value accessor
  }, {
    Header: 'URL',
    accessor: 'html_url',
  }, {
    Header: 'Owner',
    accessor: 'owner.login',
  }, {
    id: 'button',
    sortable: false,
    filterable: false,
    width: 100,
    accessor: 'full_name',
```

```
    Cell: ({value}) => (<button className="btn btn-default btn-link"
onClick=                          {() => {this.btnClick(value)}}>Press
me</button>)
  }]
```

The following is the screenshot of the table with buttons:

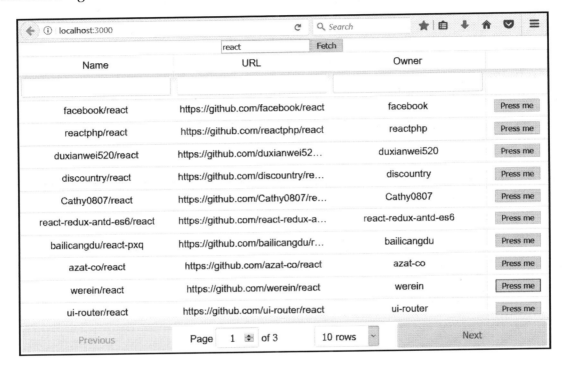

The modal window component

Modal windows are nice to have when you are creating CRUD applications. We will create a simple shopping list app where users can add new items using the modal window. The modal window component that we will use in the example is react-skylight (https://marcio.github.io/react-skylight/):

1. Create a new React app called shoppinglist and install react-skylight by using the following command:

```
npm install react-skylight --save
```

2. Open the app folder with the VS Code and open the `App.js` file in the code editor. In the `App.js` component, we need only one state to keep shopping list items. One shopping list item contains two fields—product and amount. We also need a method to add new items to the list. The following is the source code of the constructor and the method for adding new items to the list. In the `addItem` method, we are using a spread notation (. . .), which is used to add a new item at the beginning of the existing array:

```
constructor(props) {
  super(props);
  this.state={ items: [] };
}

addItem = (item) => {
  this.setState({items: [item, ...this.state.items]});
}
```

3. Add a new component for adding shopping items. Create a new file called `AddItem.js` to the root folder of the app. This component will use the React Skylight modal form so let's import `react-skylight`. Inside the React Skylight component in the `render()` method, we will add two input fields (`product` and `amount`) and a button that calls the `addItem` function. To be able to call the `addItem` function that is in the `App.js` component, we have to pass it in a prop when rendering the `AddItem` component. Outside the React Skylight component, we will add a button that opens the modal form when it is pressed. This button is the only visible element when the component is rendered initially and it calls the React Skylight `show()` method to open the modal form. We also have to handle the change event of the input fields, so that we can access the values that have been typed. When the button inside the modal form is clicked, the `addItem` function is called and the modal form is closed using the React Skylight `hide()` method. The function creates an object from the input field values and calls the `App.js` component's `addItem` function, which finally add a new item to the state array and re-renders the user interface:

```
import React, { Component } from 'react';
import SkyLight from 'react-skylight';

class AddItem extends Component {
  constructor(props) {
    super(props);
  }
  // Create new shopping item and calls addItem function.
  // Finally close the modal form
```

```
addItem = () => {
  const item = {product: this.state.product,
    amount: this.state.amount};
  this.props.additem(item);
  this.addform.hide();
}

handleChange = (e) => {
  this.setState({[e.target.name]: e.target.value});
}

render() {
  return (
    <div>
      <section>
        <button onClick={() => this.addform.show()}>Add
          Item</button>
      </section>
      <SkyLight
        hideOnOverlayClicked
        ref={ref => this.addform = ref}
        title="Add item">
        <input type="text" name="product"
          onChange={this.handleChange}
          placeholder="product" /><br/>
        <input type="text" name="amount"
          onChange={this.handleChange}
          placeholder="amount" /><br/>
        <button onClick={this.addItem}>Add</button>
      </SkyLight>
    </div>
  );
}
}

export default AddItem;
```

4. Modify the `render()` method in the `App.js` file. Add the `AddItem` component to the `render()` method and pass the `addItem` function in a prop to the `AddItem` component. At the beginning of the method, we transform items to `listItems` (`<li></li>`) using the `map` function:

```
// App.js
render() {
  const listItems = this.state.items.map((item, index) =>
    <li key={index}>{item.product} {item.amount}</li>)
```

```
        return (
          <div className="App">
            <h2>Shopping list</h2>
            <AddItem additem={this.addItem}/>
            <ul>{listItems}</ul>
          </div>
        );
      }
```

When you now open the app, you will see an empty list and a button to add new items:

When you press the **Add Item** button, the modal form opens:

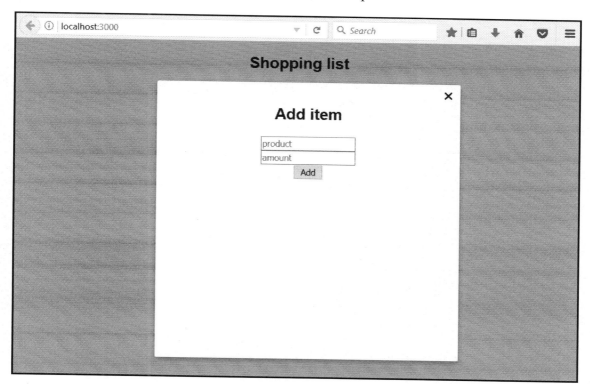

Type some values into the input boxes and press the **Add** button. The modal form is closed and the new item can be seen in the list:

Material UI component library

Material UI is the React component library that implement Google's Material Design. It contains lots of different components, such as buttons, lists, tables, and cards, which you can use to get a nice and uniform user interface. We will continue with the shopping list app and start to style the user interface with Material UI:

1. Open the shopping list app with VS Code. Install Material UI by typing the following command in the root folder to PowerShell or any suitable terminal you are using:

   ```
   npm install @material-ui/core --save
   ```

   OR with yarn

   ```
   yarn add @material-ui/core
   ```

2. We are ready to start to using the Material UI components. We will first change the buttons in the `AddItem.js` file to use the Material UI `Button` component. We have to import the `Button` component and then use it in the `render()` method. Different props of `Button` can be found in the Material UI documentation:

   ```
   // Import RaisedButton
   import RaisedButton from '@material-ui/core/Button';

   // Use RaisedButton in render() method
   render() {
     return (
       <div>
         <section>
   ```

```
        <Button onClick={() => this.addform.show()}
          variant="raised" color="primary">
          Add Item</ Button>
      </section>
      <SkyLight
        hideOnOverlayClicked
        ref={ref => this.addform = ref}
        title="Add item">
        <input type="text" name="product"
          onChange={this.handleChange}
          placeholder="product" /><br/>
        <input type="text" name="amount"
          onChange={this.handleChange}
          placeholder="amount" /><br/>
        <Button onClick={this.addItem}
          variant="default"  >Add</ Button>
      </SkyLight>
    </div>
  );
}
```

Now the app is using `RaisedButton` and it looks like this:

3. Change the input fields in `AddItem.js` to use the Material UI `TextField` component. The steps are the same as with the buttons. Import the `TextField` component and then use it in the `render()` method:

```
// Import TextField component
import TextField from '@material-ui/core/TextField';

// Use TextField in render() method
render() {
  return (
    <div>
      <section>
        <Button onClick={() => this.addform.show()}
          variant="raised" color="primary">
          Add Item</ Button>
      </section>
      <SkyLight
```

```
            hideOnOverlayClicked
            ref={ref => this.addform = ref}
            title="Add item">
            <TextField type="text" name="product"
              onChange={this.handleChange}
              placeholder="product" /><br/>
            <TextField type="text" name="amount"
              onChange={this.handleChange}
              placeholder="amount" /><br/>
            <Button onClick={this.addItem}
              variant="default"  >Add</ Button>
          </SkyLight>
        </div>
      );
    }
```

After the changes, your form should look like the following:

4. Change our list in the App.js file to use the Material UI List and ListItem
   components. Import the components and use ListItem in the map function
   where listItems are created and render List instead of ul. We will show the
   amount of the product in the secondary text of the ListItemText component:

```
// Import List, ListItem and ListItemText components
import List from '@material-ui/core/List';
import ListItem from '@material-ui/core/ListItem';
import ListItemText from '@material-ui/core/ListItemText';

// Use List and ListItem in render() method
render() {
 // Use ListItem component here instead of li
    const listItems = this.state.items.map((item, index) =>
     <ListItem key={index}>
     <ListItemText primary={item.product} secondary={item.amount}
 />
      </ListItem>)
```

```
return (
  <div className="App">
    <h2>Shopping list</h2>
    <AddItem additem={this.addItem}/>
    <List>{listItems}</List>
  </div>
);
}
```

Now the user interface looks like the following. With a small amount of work, the user interface is now much more polished:

Routing

There are multiple solutions available for routing in React. The most popular one, which we are using, is React Router (https://github.com/ReactTraining/react-router). For web applications, React Router provides a package called react-router-dom.

To start using React Router, we have to install it with the following command:

```
npm install react-router-dom --save
```

There are four different components in `react-router-dom` that are needed to implement routing. `BrowserRouter` is the router for web-based applications. The `Route` component renders the defined component if the given locations match. The following are two examples of the `Route` component. The first one renders the `Contact` component when user navigates to the `/contact` end path. You can also use inline rendering with the `Route` component, as shown in the second example:

```
<Route path="/contact" component={Contact} />
// Route with inline rendering
<Route path="/links" render={() => <h1>Links</h1>} />
```

The `Switch` component wraps multiple `Route` components. The `Link` component provides navigation to your application. The following example shows the **Contact** link and navigates to the `/contact` endpoint when the link is clicked:

```
<Link to="/contact">Contact</Link>
```

The following example shows how to use these components in practice. Let's create a new React app, called `routerapp`, using `create-react-app`. Open the app folder with VS Code and open the `App.js` file to editor view. Import components from the `react-router-dom` package and remove extra code from the render method. After the modifications, your `App.js` source code should look like the following:

```
import React, { Component } from 'react';
import './App.css';
import { BrowserRouter, Switch, Route, Link } from 'react-router-dom'

class App extends Component {
  render() {
    return (
      <div className="App">
      </div>
    );
  }
}

export default App;
```

Let's first create two simple components that we can use in routing. Create two new files, called `Home.js` and `Contact.js`, to the application root folder. Add just headers to the `render()` methods to show the name of the component. See the code of the components as follows:

```
//Contact.js
import React, { Component } from 'react';

class Contact extends Component {
  render() {
    return (
      <div>
        <h1>Contact.js</h1>
      </div>
    );
  }
}

export default Contact;

// Home.js
import React, { Component } from 'react';

class Home extends Component {
  render() {
    return (
      <div>
        <h1>Home.js</h1>
      </div>
    );
  }
}

export default Links;
```

Open the `App.js` file, and let's add a router that allows us to navigate between the components:

```
import React, { Component } from 'react';
import './App.css';
import { BrowserRouter, Switch, Route, Link } from 'react-router-dom'
import Contact from './Contact';
import Home from './Home';

class App extends Component {
  render() {
    return (
```

```
        <div className="App">
          <BrowserRouter>
            <div>
              <Link to="/">Home</Link>{' '}
              <Link to="/contact">Contact</Link>{' '}
              <Link to="/links">Links</Link>{' '}
              <Switch>
                <Route exact path="/" component={Home} />
                <Route path="/contact" component={Contact} />
                <Route path="/links" render={() => <h1>Links</h1>} />
                <Route render={() => <h1>Page not found</h1>} />
              </Switch>
            </div>
          </BrowserRouter>
        </div>
      );
    }
  }

  export default App;
```

Now, when you start the app, you will see the links and the Home component, which is shown in the root end path (localhost:3030/) as defined in the first Route component. The exact keyword in the first Route component means that the path must match exactly. If you remove that, then the routing always goes to the Home component:

When you press the **Contact** link, the Contact component is rendered:

Summary

In this chapter, we learned how to use third-party React components. We familiarized ourselves with several components that we are going to use in our frontend. React Table is the table component with built-in features, such as sorting, paging, and filtering. React Skylight is the modal form component that we will use in our frontend to create forms for adding and editing items. Material UI is the component library that provides multiple user interface components that implement Google's Material Design. We also learned how to use React Router for routing in React applications. In the next chapter we will build an environment for the frontend development.

Questions

1. How should you find components for React?
2. How should you install components?
3. How should you use the React Table component?
4. How should you create modal forms with React?
5. How should you use the Material UI component library?
6. How should you implement routing in a React application?

Further reading

Packt has other great resources for learning about React:

- https://www.packtpub.com/web-development/getting-started-react
- https://www.packtpub.com/web-development/react-16-essentials-second-edition

Setting Up the Frontend for Our Spring Boot RESTful Web Service

9

This chapter explains the steps that are needed to start the development of the frontend part. We will first define the functionalities that we are developing. Then we will do the mock-up of the user interface. As a backend, we will use our Spring Boot application from Chapter 4, *Securing and Testing Your Backend*. We will start development using the unsecured version of the backend. Finally, we will create the React app that we will use in our frontend development.

In this chapter, we will look at the following:

- Why and how to do a mock-up
- Preparing our Spring Boot backend for frontend development
- Creating the React app for the frontend

Technical requirements

The Spring Boot application that we created in Chapter 4, *Securing and Testing Your Backend* is needed.

Node.js and `create-react-app` should be installed.

Mocking up the user interface

In the first few chapters of this book, we created a car database backend that provides the REST API. Now it is time to start building the frontend to our application. We will create a frontend that list cars from the database and provides paging, sorting, and filtering. There is a button that opens the modal form to add new cars to the database. In each row of the car table, there is a button to delete the car from the database. Table rows are also editable and modifications can be saved to the database by clicking the **Save** button in the row. The frontend contains a link or button to export data from the table to a CSV file.

Let's create a mock-up from our user interface. There are lots of different applications for creating mock-ups, or you could even use a pencil and paper. You can also create interactive mock-ups to demonstrate some functionalities. If you have done the mock-up, it is much easier to discuss needs with the client before you start to write any actual code. With the mock-up, it is also easier for the client to understand the idea of the frontend and affect to it. Changes to the mock-up are really easy and fast to do, compared to modifications with real frontend source code.

The following screenshot shows the mock-up of our car list frontend:

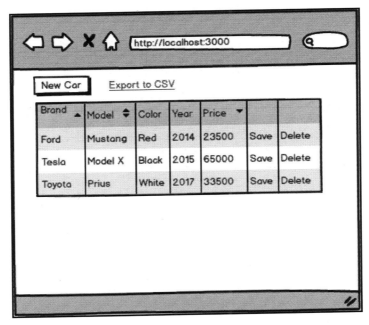

The modal form that is opened when the user press **New Car** button looks like the following:

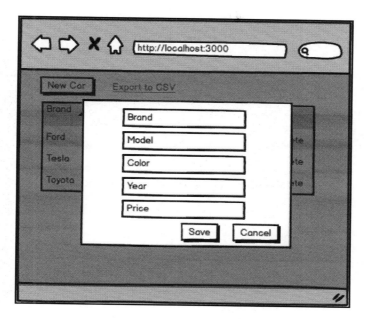

Preparing the Spring Boot backend

We are starting the frontend development with the unsecured version of our backend. In the first phase, we implement all CRUD functionalities and test that these are working correctly. In the second phase, we enable security in our backend and make the modifications that are needed, and finally we implement authentication.

Open the Spring Boot application with Eclipse, which we created in `Chapter 4`, *Securing and Testing Your Backend*. Open the `SecurityConfig.java` file that defines the Spring Security configuration. Temporarily comment out the current configuration and give everyone access to all endpoints. See the following modifications:

```
@Override
protected void configure(HttpSecurity http) throws Exception {
  // Add this row to allow access to all endpoints
  http.cors().and().authorizeRequests().anyRequest().permitAll();
  /* Comment this out
  http.cors().and().authorizeRequests()
    .antMatchers(HttpMethod.POST, "/login").permitAll()
```

```
        .anyRequest().authenticated()
    .and()
    // Filter for the api/login requests
    .addFilterBefore(new LoginFilter("/login", authenticationManager()),
            UsernamePasswordAuthenticationFilter.class)
    // Filter for other requests to check JWT in header
    .addFilterBefore(new AuthenticationFilter(),
     UsernamePasswordAuthenticationFilter.class);
    */
    }
```

Now, if you run the backend and test the `http:/localhost:8080/api/cars` endpoint with Postman, you should get all cars in the response, as shown in the following screenshot:

Creating the React project for the frontend

Before we start coding the frontend, we have to create a new React app:

1. Open the PowerShell or any other suitable terminal. Create a new React app by typing the following command:

   ```
   create-react-app carfront
   ```

2. Run the app by typing the following command:

   ```
   npm start
   ```

   Or, if you are using Yarn, type in the following:

   ```
   yarn start
   ```

3. Open the app folder with VS Code, remove any extra code, and change the header text from the App.js file. After the modifications, your App.js file source code should look as follows:

   ```
   import React, { Component } from 'react';
   import './App.css';

   class App extends Component {
     render() {
       return (
         <div className="App">
           <header className="App-header">
             <h1 className="App-title">CarList</h1>
           </header>
         </div>
       );
     }
   }

   export default App;
   ```

4. Let's also decrease the header height and change the color to lightblue. Open the App.css file where you can find stylings of the App.js file. Decrease the header height from 150 to 50 and change the color to lightblue:

```
.App-header {
  background-color:lightblue;
  height: 50px;
  padding: 20px;
  color: white;
}
```

Now your frontend starting point should look like the following:

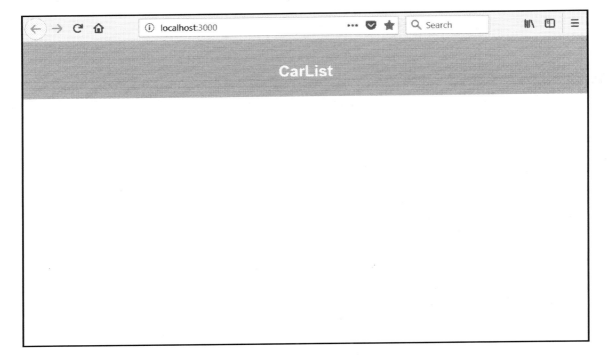

Summary

In this chapter, we started the development of our frontend, using the backend that we created in Chapter 4, *Securing and Testing Your Backend*. We defined the functionalities of the frontend and created a mock-up of the user interface. We started frontend development with an unsecured version of the backend, therefore, we made some modifications to our Spring Security configuration class. We also created the React app that we are going to use during development. In the next chapter, we will start to add CRUD functionalities to our frontend.

Questions

1. Why should you do a mock-up of the user interface?
2. How should you do a mock-up?
3. How should you disable Spring Security from the backend?

Further reading

Packt has other great resources for learning about React:

- https://www.packtpub.com/web-development/getting-started-react
- https://www.packtpub.com/web-development/react-16-essentials-second-edition

10
Adding CRUD Functionalities

This chapter describes how to implement CRUD functionalities to our frontend. We are going to use the components that we learned about in Chapter 8, *Useful Third-Party Components for React*. We will fetch data from our backend and present the data in a table. Then, we will implement delete, edit, and add functionalities. In the final part, we will add features to export data to a CSV file.

In this chapter, we will look at the following:

- How to fetch data from the backend and present it in the frontend
- How to delete, add, and update data using the REST API
- How to show toast messages to the user
- How to export data to the CSV file from the React app

Technical requirements

The Spring Boot application that we created in Chapter 4, *Securing and Testing Your Backend* is needed with the modification from the previous chapter (the unsecured backend).

We also need the React app that we created in the previous chapter (*carfront*).

Creating the list page

In the first phase, we will create the list page to show cars with paging, filtering, and sorting features. Run your Spring Boot backend, the cars can be fetched by sending the GET request to the http://localhost:8080/api/cars URL, as shown in Chapter 3, *Creating a RESTful Web Service with Spring Boot*.

Let's inspect the JSON data from the response. The array of cars can be found in the
`_embedded.cars` node of the JSON response data:

```
GET  ∨        http://localhost:8080/api/cars

Body    Cookies (1)    Headers (9)    Test Results

Pretty    Raw    Preview    JSON ∨   ⇉

  1 ▾ {
  2 ▾     "_embedded": {
  3 ▾         "cars": [
  4 ▾             {
  5                 "brand": "Ford",
  6                 "model": "Mustang",
  7                 "color": "Red",
  8                 "registerNumber": "ADF-1121",
  9                 "year": 2017,
 10                 "price": 59000,
 11 ▾             "_links": {
 12 ▾                 "self": {
 13                         "href": "http://localhost:8080/api/cars/3"
 14                     },
 15 ▾                 "car": {
 16                         "href": "http://localhost:8080/api/cars/3"
 17                     },
 18 ▾                 "owner": {
 19                         "href": "http://localhost:8080/api/cars/3/owner"
 20                     }
 21                 }
 22             },
 23 ▾             {
 24                 "brand": "Nissan",
 25                 "model": "Leaf",
 26                 "color": "White",
 27                 "registerNumber": "SSJ-3002",
```

Now, once we know how to fetch cars from the backend, we are ready to implement the list
page to show the cars. The following steps describe this in practice:

1. Open the *carfront* React app with the VS Code (the React app created in the
   previous chapter).

2. When the app has multiple components, it is recommended to create a folder for
   them. Create a new folder, called `components`, in the `src` folder. With the VS
   Code, you can create a folder by right-clicking the folder in the sidebar file
   explorer and selecting **New Folder** from the menu:

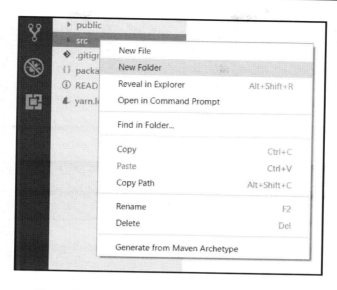

3. Create a new file, called `Carlist.js`, in the `components` folder and now your project structure should look like the following:

4. Open the `Carlist.js` file in the editor view and write the base code of the component, shown as follows:

```
import React, { Component } from 'react';

class Carlist extends Component {
  render() {
    return (
      <div></div>
    );
  }
}

export default Carlist;
```

5. We need a state for the `cars` that are fetched from the REST API, therefore, we have to add the constructor and define one array-type state value:

```
constructor(props) {
  super(props);
  this.state = { cars: []};
}
```

6. Execute `fetch` in the `componentDidMount()` life cycle method. The cars from the JSON response data will be saved to the state, called `cars`:

```
componentDidMount() {
  fetch('http://localhost:8080/api/cars')
  .then((response) => response.json())
  .then((responseData) => {
    this.setState({
      cars: responseData._embedded.cars,
    });
  })
  .catch(err => console.error(err));
}
```

7. Use the map function to transform `car` objects into table rows in the `render()` method and add the table element:

```
render() {
  const tableRows = this.state.cars.map((car, index) =>
    <tr key={index}>
      <td>{car.brand}</td>
      <td>{car.model}</td>
      <td>{car.color}</td>
      <td>{car.year}</td>
```

```
                <td>{car.price}</td>
            </tr>
        );

        return (
            <div className="App">
                <table>
                    <tbody>{tableRows}</tbody>
                </table>
            </div>
        );
    }
```

Now, if you start the React app with the `npm start` command, you should see the following list page:

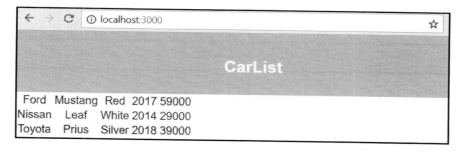

The URL server can repeat multiple times when we create more CRUD functionalities, and it will change when the backend is deployed to a server other than the localhost. Therefore, it is better to define it as a constant. Then, when the URL value changes, we have to modify it only in one place. Let's create a new file, called `constants.js`, in the root folder of our app. Open the file in the editor and add the following line into the file:

```
export const SERVER_URL = 'http://localhost:8080/'
```

Then, we will import it to our `Carlist.js` file and use it in the `fetch` method:

```
//Carlist.js
// Import server url (named import)
import {SERVER_URL} from '../constants.js'

// Use imported constant in the fetch method
fetch(SERVER_URL + 'api/cars')
```

Finally, your `Carlist.js` file source code should look like the following:

```
import React, { Component } from 'react';
import {SERVER_URL} from '../constants.js'

class Carlist extends Component {
  constructor(props) {
    super(props);
    this.state = { cars: []};
  }

  componentDidMount() {
    fetch(SERVER_URL + 'api/cars')
    .then((response) => response.json())
    .then((responseData) => {
      this.setState({
        cars: responseData._embedded.cars,
      });
    })
    .catch(err => console.error(err));
  }
  render() {
    const tableRows = this.state.cars.map((car, index) =>
      <tr key={index}><td>{car.brand}</td>
       <td>{car.model}</td><td>{car.color}</td>
       <td>{car.year}</td><td>{car.price}</td></tr>);

    return (
      <div className="App">
        <table><tbody>{tableRows}</tbody></table>
      </div>
    );
  }
}

export default Carlist;
```

Now we will use React Table to get the paging, filtering, and sorting features out of the box. Stop the development server by pressing *Ctrl* + *C* in the terminal, and type the following command to install React Table. After the installation, restart the app:

```
npm install react-table --save
```

Import `react-table` and the style sheet to your `Carlist.js` file:

```
import ReactTable from "react-table";
import 'react-table/react-table.css';
```

Then remove `table` and `tableRows` from the `render()` method. The `data` prop of React Table is `this.state.cars`, which contains fetched cars. We also have to define the `columns` of the table, where `accessor` is the field of the `car` object and `header` is the text of the header. To enable filtering, we set the `filterable` prop of the table to `true`. See the source code of the following `render()` method:

```
render() {
  const columns = [{
    Header: 'Brand',
    accessor: 'brand'
  }, {
    Header: 'Model',
    accessor: 'model',
  }, {
    Header: 'Color',
    accessor: 'color',
  }, {
    Header: 'Year',
    accessor: 'year',
  }, {
    Header: 'Price €',
    accessor: 'price',
  },]

  return (
    <div className="App">
      <ReactTable data={this.state.cars} columns={columns}
        filterable={true}/>
    </div>
  );
}
```

With the React Table component, we acquired all the necessary features to our table with a small amount of coding. Now the list page looks like the following:

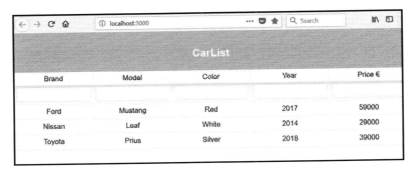

The delete functionality

Items can be deleted from the database by sending the DELETE method request to the `http://localhost:8080/api/cars/[carid]` endpoint. If we look at the JSON response data, we can see that each car contains a link to itself and it can be accessed from the `_links.self.href` node, as shown in the following screenshot:

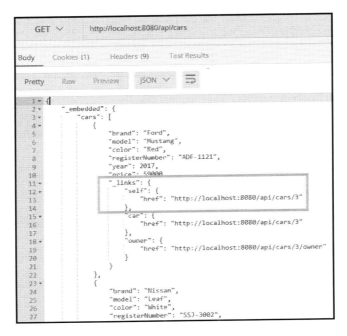

The following steps show how to implement delete functionality:

1. We will create a button for each row in the table and the accessor of the button will be _links.self.href, which we can use to call the delete function that we will create soon. But first, add a new column to the table using Cell to render the button. See the following source code. We don't want to enable sorting and filtering for the button column, therefore these props are set to be false. The button invokes the onDelClick function when pressed and sends a link to the car as an argument:

```
const columns = [{
  Header: 'Brand',
  accessor: 'brand'
}, {
  Header: 'Model',
  accessor: 'model',
}, {
  Header: 'Color',
  accessor: 'color',
}, {
  Header: 'Year',
  accessor: 'year',
}, {
  Header: 'Price €',
  accessor: 'price',
}, {
  id: 'delbutton',
  sortable: false,
  filterable: false,
  width: 100,
  accessor: '_links.self.href',
  Cell: ({value}) => (<button
onClick={()=>{this.onDelClick(value)}}>Delete</button>)
}]
```

2. Implement the `onDelClick` function. But first, let's take the `fetchCars` function out from the `componentDidMount()` method. That is needed because we want to call the `fetchCars` function also after the car has been deleted to show an updated list of the cars to the user. Create a new function, called `fetchCars()`, and copy the code from the `componentDidMount()` method into a new function. Then call the `fetchCars()` function from the `componentDidMount()` function to fetch cars initially:

```
componentDidMount() {
  this.fetchCars();
}

fetchCars = () => {
  fetch(SERVER_URL + 'api/cars')
  .then((response) => response.json())
  .then((responseData) => {
    this.setState({
      cars: responseData._embedded.cars,
    });
  })
  .catch(err => console.error(err));
}
```

3. Implement the `onDelClick` function. We send the DELETE request to a car link, and when the delete succeeds, we refresh the list page by calling the `fetchCars()` function:

```
// Delete car
onDelClick = (link) => {
  fetch(link, {method: 'DELETE'})
  .then(res => this.fetchCars())
  .catch(err => console.error(err))
}
```

When you start your app, the frontend should look like the following screenshot, and the car disappears from the list when the **Delete** button is pressed:

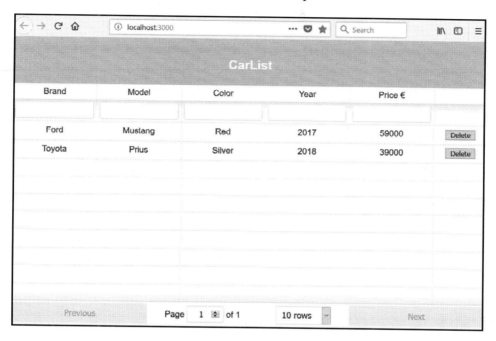

It would be nice to show the user some feedback upon successful deletion or if there are any errors. Let's implement a toast message to show the status of deletion. For that, we are going to use the react-toastify component (https://github.com/fkhadra/react-toastify). Install the component by typing the following command into the terminal you are using:

```
npm install react-toastify --save
```

After the installation is complete, start your app and open the Carlist.js file in the editor. We have to import ToastContainer, toast, and the style sheet to start using react-toastify. Add the following import statements to your Carlist.js file:

```
import { ToastContainer, toast } from 'react-toastify';
import 'react-toastify/dist/ReactToastify.css';
```

`ToastContainer` is the container component for showing toast messages, and it should be inside the `render()` method. In `ToastContainer`, you can define the duration of the toast message in milliseconds using the `autoClose` prop. Add the `ToastContainer` component inside the return statement in the `render()` method, just after `ReactTable`:

```
return (
  <div className="App">
    <ReactTable data={this.state.cars} columns={columns}
      filterable={true}/>
    <ToastContainer autoClose={1500} } />
  </div>
);
```

Then, we will call the toast method in the `onDelClick()` function to show the toast message. You can define the type and position of the message. The success message is shown when deletion succeeds, and the error message is shown in the case of an error:

```
// Delete car
onDelClick = (link) => {
  fetch(link, {method: 'DELETE'})
  .then(res => {
    toast.success("Car deleted", {
      position: toast.POSITION.BOTTOM_LEFT
    });
    this.fetchCars();
  })
  .catch(err => {
    toast.error("Error when deleting", {
      position: toast.POSITION.BOTTOM_LEFT
    });
    console.error(err)
  })
}
```

Now you will see the toast message when the car has been deleted, as shown in the following screenshot:

To avoid accidental deletion of the car, it would be nice to have a confirmation dialog after the delete button has been pressed. We will implement this using the `react-confirm-alert` component (https://github.com/GA-MO/react-confirm-alert). If your app is running, stop the development server by pressing *Ctrl + C* in the terminal and type the following command to install `react-confirm-alert`. After installation, restart the app:

```
npm install react-confirm-alert --save
```

Import `confirmAlert` and the CSS file to the `Carlist` component:

```
import { confirmAlert } from 'react-confirm-alert';
import 'react-confirm-alert/src/react-confirm-alert.css'
```

Create a new function, called `confirmDelete`, that opens the confirmation dialog. If the **Yes** button of the dialog is pressed, the `onDelClick` function is called and the car will be deleted:

```
confirmDelete = (link) => {
  confirmAlert({
    message: 'Are you sure to delete?',
    buttons: [
      {
```

```
        label: 'Yes',
        onClick: () => this.onDelClick(link)
      },
      {
        label: 'No',
      }
    ]
  })
}
```

Then, change the function in the **Delete** button's `onClick` event to `confirmDelete`:

```
render() {
  const columns = [{
    Header: 'Brand',
    accessor: 'brand',
  }, {
    Header: 'Model',
    accessor: 'model',
  }, {
    Header: 'Color',
    accessor: 'color',
  }, {
    Header: 'Year',
    accessor: 'year',
  }, {
    Header: 'Price €',
    accessor: 'price',
  }, {
    id: 'delbutton',
    sortable: false,
    filterable: false,
    width: 100,
    accessor: '_links.self.href',
    Cell: ({value}) => (<button onClick=
      {()=>{this.confirmDelete(value)}}>Delete</button>)
  }]
```

If you now press the **Delete** button, the confirmation dialog will be opened and the car will be deleted only if you press the **Yes** button:

The add functionality

The next step is to create an add functionality for the frontend. We will implement that using the React Skylight modal component. We already went through the usage of React Skylight in Chapter 8, *Useful Third-Party React Components for React*. We will add the **New Car** button to the user interface, which opens the modal form when it is pressed. The modal form contains all the fields that are required to save the car as well as the button for saving and canceling.

Stop the development server by pressing *Ctrl + C* in the terminal, and type the following command to install React Skylight. After installation, restart the app:

```
npm install react-skylight --save
```

The following steps show how to create add functionality using the modal form component:

1. Create a new file, called `AddCar.js`, in the `components` folder and write a component-class base code to the file, as shown here. Add the import for the `react-skylight` component:

```
import React from 'react';
import SkyLight from 'react-skylight';

class AddCar extends React.Component {
  render() {
    return (
      <div>
      </div>
    );
  }
}

export default AddCar;
```

2. Introduce a state that contains all car fields:

```
constructor(props) {
    super(props);
    this.state = {brand: '', model: '', year: '', color: '', price:
'' };
}
```

3. Add a form inside the `render()` method. The form contains the `ReactSkylight` modal form component with buttons and the input fields that are needed to collect the car data. The button that opens the modal window, and will be shown in the carlist page, must be outside `ReactSkylight`. All input fields should have the `name` attribute with a value that is the same as the name of the state the value will be saved to. Input fields also have the `onChange` handler, which saves the value to state by invoking the `handleChange` function:

```
handleChange = (event) => {
    this.setState(
      {[event.target.name]: event.target.value}
    );
}
render() {
    return (
      <div>
        <SkyLight hideOnOverlayClicked ref="addDialog">
```

```
      <h3>New car</h3>
      <form>
        <input type="text" placeholder="Brand" name="brand"
          onChange={this.handleChange}/><br/>
        <input type="text" placeholder="Model" name="model"
          onChange={this.handleChange}/><br/>
        <input type="text" placeholder="Color" name="color"
          onChange={this.handleChange}/><br/>
        <input type="text" placeholder="Year" name="year"
          onChange={this.handleChange}/><br/>
        <input type="text" placeholder="Price" name="price"
          onChange={this.handleChange}/><br/>
        <button onClick={this.handleSubmit}>Save</button>
        <button onClick={this.cancelSubmit}>Cancel</button>
      </form>
    </SkyLight>
    <div>
      <button style={{'margin': '10px'}}
        onClick={() => this.refs.addDialog.show()}>New
car</button>
    </div>
  </div>
);
```

4. Insert the `AddCar` component to the `Carlist` component to see whether that form can be opened. Open the `Carlist.js` file to editor view and import the `AddCar` component:

```
import AddCar from './AddCar.js';
```

5. Implement the `addCar` function to the `Carlist.js` file that will send the POST request to the backend `api/cars` endpoint. The request will include the new `car` object inside the body and the `'Content-Type': 'application/json'` header. The header is needed because the `car` object is converted to JSON format using the `JSON.stringify()` method:

```
// Add new car
addCar(car) {
  fetch(SERVER_URL + 'api/cars',
    { method: 'POST',
      headers: {
        'Content-Type': 'application/json',
      },
      body: JSON.stringify(car)
    })
  .then(res => this.fetchCars())
```

```
        .catch(err => console.error(err))
    }
```

6. Add the `AddCar` component to the `render()` method and pass the `addCar` and `fetchCars` functions as props to the `AddCar` component that allows us to call these functions from the `AddCar` component. Now the return statement of the `CarList.js` file should look like the following:

```
// Carlist.js
return (
  <div className="App">
    <AddCar addCar={this.addCar} fetchCars={this.fetchCars}/>
    <ReactTable data={this.state.cars} columns={columns}
      filterable={true} pageSize={10}/>
    <ToastContainer autoClose={1500}/>
  </div>
);
```

If you start the frontend app, it should now look like the following, and if you press the **New Car** button, it should open the modal form:

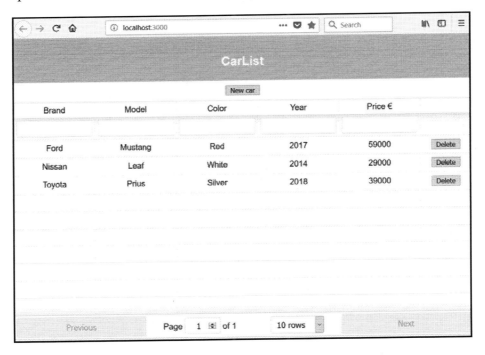

7. Implement the `handleSubmit` and `cancelSubmit` functions to the `AddCar.js` file. The `handleSubmit` function creates a new `car` object and calls the `addCar` function, which can be accessed using props. The `cancelSubmit` function just closes the modal form:

```
// Save car and close modal form
handleSubmit = (event) => {
   event.preventDefault();
   var newCar = {brand: this.state.brand, model: this.state.model,
     color: this.state.color, year: this.state.year,
     price: this.state.price};
   this.props.addCar(newCar);
   this.refs.addDialog.hide();
}

// Cancel and close modal form
cancelSubmit = (event) => {
  event.preventDefault();
  this.refs.addDialog.hide();
}
```

Now, you can open the modal form by pressing the **New Car** button. Then you can fill the form with data, and press the **Save** button. So far, the form does not look nice, but we are going to style it in the next chapter:

The list page is refreshed, and the new car can be seen in the list:

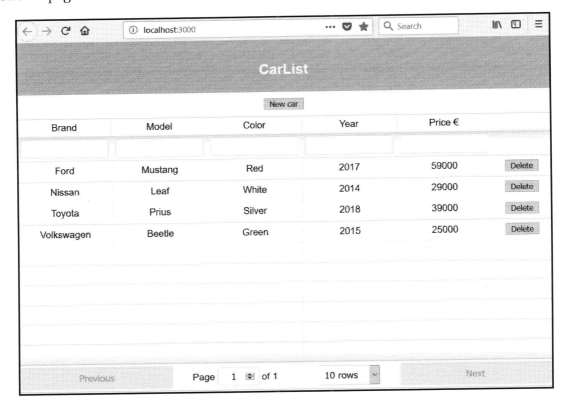

The edit functionality

We will implement the edit functionality by changing the table to editable and adding the save button to each row. The save button will invoke the function that sends the PUT request to the backend for saving the changes to the database:

1. Add the cell renderer, which changes the table cells to editable. Open the
   `Carlist.js` file and create a new function called `renderEditable`. See the
   source code for the following function. The cell will be the `div` element and the
   `contentEditable` attribute makes it editable.
   `suppressContentEditableWarning` suppresses the warning that comes when
   the element with the child is marked to be editable. The function in `onBlur` is
   executed when the user leaves the table cell, and this is where we will update the
   state:

```
renderEditable = (cellInfo) => {
  return (
    <div
      style={{ backgroundColor: "#fafafa" }}
      contentEditable
      suppressContentEditableWarning
      onBlur={e => {
        const data = [...this.state.cars];
        data[cellInfo.index][cellInfo.column.id] =
          e.target.innerHTML;
        this.setState({ cars: data });
      }}
      dangerouslySetInnerHTML={{
        __html: this.state.cars[cellInfo.index][cellInfo.column.id]
      }}
    />
  );
}
```

2. Define the table columns that are going to be editable. This is done using the
   `Cell` attribute of the column in React Table, which defines how the cell of the
   column will be rendered:

```
const columns = [{
  Header: 'Brand',
  accessor: 'brand',
  Cell: this.renderEditable
}, {
  Header: 'Model',
  accessor: 'model',
  Cell: this.renderEditable
}, {
  Header: 'Color',
  accessor: 'color',
  Cell: this.renderEditable
}, {
  Header: 'Year',
```

```
      accessor: 'year',
      Cell: this.renderEditable
}, {
    Header: 'Price €',
    accessor: 'price',
    Cell: this.renderEditable
}, {
    id: 'delbutton',
    sortable: false,
    filterable: false,
    width: 100,
    accessor: '_links.self.href',
    Cell: ({value}) => (<button
onClick={()=>{this.onDelClick(value)}}>Delete</button>)
}]
```

Now, if you open the app in your browser, you can see that the table cells are editable:

3. To update car data, we have to send the PUT request to the
   `http://localhost:8080/api/cars/[carid]` URL. The link will be the same
   as with the delete functionality. The request contains the updated `car` object
   inside the body, and the `'Content-Type': 'application/json'` header that
   we had in the add functionality. Create a new function, called `updateCar`, and
   the source code of the function is shown in the following code snippet. The
   function gets two arguments, the updated `car` object and the request URL. After
   the successful update, we will show a toast message to the user:

```
// Update car
updateCar(car, link) {
  fetch(link,
  { method: 'PUT',
    headers: {
      'Content-Type': 'application/json',
    },
    body: JSON.stringify(car)
  })
  .then( res =>
    toast.success("Changes saved", {
      position: toast.POSITION.BOTTOM_LEFT
    })
  )
  .catch( err =>
    toast.error("Error when saving", {
      position: toast.POSITION.BOTTOM_LEFT
    })
  )
}
```

4. Add the **Save** button to the table rows. When the user presses the button, it calls
   the `updateCar` function and passes two arguments. The first argument is `row`,
   which is all values in the row as an `object` (=car object). The second
   argument is `value`, which is set to be `_links.href.self`, which will be the
   URL of the car that we need in the request:

```
const columns = [{
  Header: 'Brand',
  accessor: 'brand',
  Cell: this.renderEditable
}, {
  Header: 'Model',
  accessor: 'model',
  Cell: this.renderEditable
}, {
```

```
      Header: 'Color',
      accessor: 'color',
      Cell: this.renderEditable
    }, {
      Header: 'Year',
      accessor: 'year',
      Cell: this.renderEditable
    }, {
      Header: 'Price €',
      accessor: 'price',
      Cell: this.renderEditable
    }, {
      id: 'savebutton',
      sortable: false,
      filterable: false,
      width: 100,
      accessor: '_links.self.href',
      Cell: ({value, row}) =>
        (<button onClick={()=>{this.updateCar(row, value)}}>
        Save</button>)
    }, {
      id: 'delbutton',
      sortable: false,
      filterable: false,
      width: 100,
      accessor: '_links.self.href',
      Cell: ({value}) => (<button onClick=
        {()=>{this.onDelClick(value)}}>Delete</button>)
    }]
```

If you now edit the values in the table and press the Save button, you should see the toast message and the updated values are saved to the database:

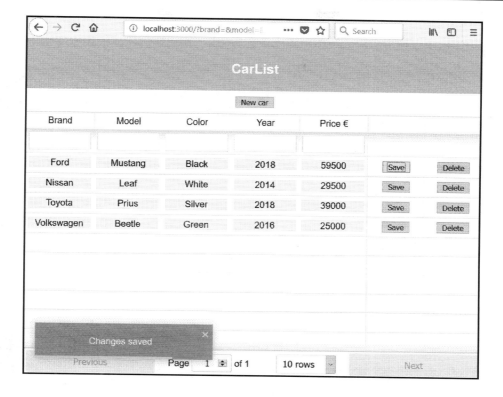

Other functionalities

One feature that we will also implement is a CSV export of the data. There is package, called `react-csv` (https://github.com/abdennour/react-csv), that can be used to export an array of data to the CSV file.

If your app is started, stop the development server by pressing *Ctrl + C* in the terminal, and type the following command to install `react-csv`. After installation, restart the app:

```
npm install react-csv --save
```

The `react-csv` package contains two components—`CSVLink` and `CSVDownload`. We will use the first one in our app, so add the following import to the `Carlist.js` file:

```
import { CSVLink } from 'react-csv';
```

The CSVLink component takes the data prop, which contains the data array that will be exported to the CSV file. You can also define the data separator using the separator prop (the default separator is a comma). Add the CSVLink component inside the return statement in the render() method. The value of the data prop will now be this.state.cars:

```
// Carlist.js render() method
return (
  <div className="App">
    <CSVLink data={this.state.cars} separator=";">Export CSV</CSVLink>
    <AddCar addCar={this.addCar} fetchCars={this.fetchCars}/>
    <ReactTable data={this.state.cars} columns={columns}
        filterable={true} pageSize={10}/>
    <ToastContainer autoClose={6500}/>
  </div>
);
```

Open the app in your browser and you should see the **Export CSV** link in our app. The styling is not nice, but we will handle that in the next chapter. If you press the link, you will get the data in the CSV file:

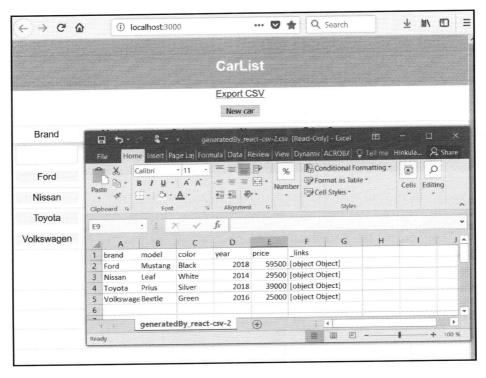

Now all the functionalities have been implemented.

Summary

In this chapter, we implemented all the functionalities for our app. We started with fetching the cars from the backend and showing these in React Table, which provides paging, sorting, and filtering features. Then we implemented the delete functionality and used the toast component to give feedback to the user. The add functionality was implemented using the React Skylight modal-form component. In the edit functionality, we utilized the React Table feature that makes tables editable. Finally, we implemented the ability to export data to a CSV file. In the next chapter, we will start to polish our user interface using the Material UI component library. In the next chapter, we are styling our frontend using React Material-UI component library.

Questions

1. How should you fetch and present data using the REST API with React?
2. How should you delete data using the REST API with React?
3. How should you add data using the REST API with React?
4. How should you update data using the REST API with React?
5. How should you show toast messages with React?
6. How should you export data to a CSV file with React?

Further reading

Packt has other great resources for learning about React:

- https://www.packtpub.com/web-development/getting-started-react
- https://www.packtpub.com/web-development/react-16-essentials-second-edition

Styling the Frontend with React Material-UI

11

This chapter explains how to use Material-UI components in our frontend. We will use the `Button` component to show the styled buttons. The modal form input fields are replaced by `TextField` components, which have many nice features. Material-UI provides the `Snackbar` component, which can show the toast messages to an end user. We replace the `react-toastify` component with `Snackbar` to get a uniform outlook. Finally, we use the `AppBar` component instead of the React app header.

In this chapter, we will look at the following:

- What is Material-UI?
- How to use Material-UI components in our frontend
- How to remove unused components in the React app

Technical requirements

The Spring Boot application that we created in Chapter 4, *Securing and Testing Your Backend*, is needed with the modification from the previous chapter (the unsecured backend).

We also need the React app that we used in the previous chapter (*carfront*).

Using the Button component

Install Material-UI by typing the following command into the terminal you are using and starting your app after the installation is finished:

```
npm install @material-ui/core --save
```

Let's first change all the buttons to use the Material-UI Button component. Import the Button to the AddCar.js file:

```
// AddCar.js
import Button from '@material-ui/core/Button';
```

Change the buttons to use the Button component. In the list page, we are using the primary button and in the modal form, the outline buttons:

```
render() {
  return (
    <div>
      <SkyLight hideOnOverlayClicked ref="addDialog">
        <h3>New car</h3>
        <form>
          <input type="text" placeholder="Brand" name="brand"
          onChange={this.handleChange}/><br/>
          <input type="text" placeholder="Model" name="model"
          onChange={this.handleChange}/><br/>
          <input type="text" placeholder="Color" name="color"
          onChange={this.handleChange}/><br/>
          <input type="text" placeholder="Year" name="year"
          onChange={this.handleChange}/><br/>
          <input type="text" placeholder="Price" name="price"
          onChange={this.handleChange}/><br/><br/>
          <Button variant="outlined" color="primary"
          onClick={this.handleSubmit}>Save</Button>
          <Button variant="outlined" color="secondary"
          onClick={this.cancelSubmit}>Cancel</Button>
        </form>
      </SkyLight>
      <div>
          <Button variant="raised" color="primary"
          style={{'margin': '10px'}}
          onClick={() => this.refs.addDialog.show()}>
          New Car</Button>
      </div>
    </div>
  );
```

Now, the list page button should look like the following:

And the modal form buttons should look like the following:

We use the flat variant buttons in the car table and define the button size as small. See the following source code for the table columns:

```
// Carlist.js render() method
const columns = [{
  Header: 'Brand',
  accessor: 'brand',
  Cell: this.renderEditable
}, {
  Header: 'Model',
  accessor: 'model',
  Cell: this.renderEditable
}, {
```

```
   Header: 'Color',
   accessor: 'color',
   Cell: this.renderEditable
}, {
   Header: 'Year',
   accessor: 'year',
   Cell: this.renderEditable
}, {
   Header: 'Price €',
   accessor: 'price',
   Cell: this.renderEditable
}, {
   id: 'savebutton',
   sortable: false,
   filterable: false,
   width: 100,
   accessor: '_links.self.href',
   Cell: ({value, row}) => (<Button size="small" variant="flat"
color="primary"
      onClick={()=>{this.updateCar(row, value)}}>Save</Button>)
}, {
   id: 'delbutton',
   sortable: false,
   filterable: false,
   width: 100,
   accessor: '_links.self.href',
   Cell: ({value}) => (<Button size="small" variant="flat" color="secondary"
      onClick={()=>{this.confirmDelete(value)}}>Delete</Button>)
}]
```

Now, the table should look like the following:

Brand	Model	Color	Year	Price €		
Ford	Mustang	Red	2017	59000	SAVE	DELETE
Nissan	Leaf	White	2014	29000	SAVE	DELETE
Toyota	Prius	Silver	2018	39000	SAVE	DELETE

Using the Grid component

Material-UI provides a `Grid` component that can be used to get a grid layout to your React app. We will use `Grid` to get **New Item** button and the **Export CSV** link on the same line.

Add the following import to the `Carlist.js` file to import the `Grid` component:

```
import Grid from '@material-ui/core/Grid';
```

Next, we wrap `AddCar` and `CSVLink` inside the `Grid` components. There are two types of `Grid` components—a container and an item. Both components are wrapped inside the item's `Grid` components. Then both items' `Grid` components are wrapped inside the container's `Grid` component:

```
// Carlist.js render() method
return (
  <div className="App">
    <Grid container>
      <Grid item>
        <AddCar addCar={this.addCar} fetchCars={this.fetchCars}/>
      </Grid>
      <Grid item style={{padding: 20}}>
        <CSVLink data={this.state.cars} separator=";">Export CSV</CSVLink>
      </Grid>
    </Grid>

    <ReactTable data={this.state.cars} columns={columns}
      filterable={true} pageSize={10}/>
    <ToastContainer autoClose={1500}/>
  </div>
);
```

Now, your app should look like the following and the buttons are now placed in one row:

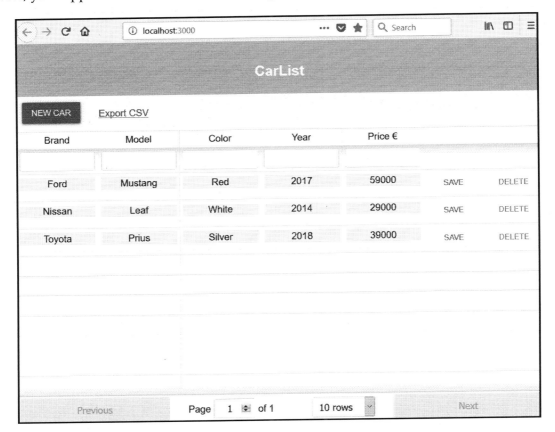

Using the TextField components

In this section, we'll change the text input in the modal form using the Material-UI `TextField` component. Add the following import statement to the `AddCar.js` file:

```
import TextField from '@material-ui/core/TextField';
```

Then, change the input to the `TextField` components in the form. We are using the `label` props to set the labels of the `TextField` components:

```
render() {
  return (
    <div>
      <SkyLight hideOnOverlayClicked ref="addDialog">
        <h3>New car</h3>
        <form>
          <TextField label="Brand" placeholder="Brand"
            name="brand" onChange={this.handleChange}/><br/>
          <TextField label="Model" placeholder="Model"
            name="model" onChange={this.handleChange}/><br/>
          <TextField label="Color" placeholder="Color"
            name="color" onChange={this.handleChange}/><br/>
          <TextField label="Year" placeholder="Year"
            name="year" onChange={this.handleChange}/><br/>
          <TextField label="Price" placeholder="Price"
            name="price" onChange={this.handleChange}/><br/><br/>
          <Button variant="outlined" color="primary"
            onClick={this.handleSubmit}>Save</Button>
          <Button variant="outlined" color="secondary"
            onClick={this.cancelSubmit}>Cancel</Button>
        </form>
      </SkyLight>
      <div>
        <Button variant="raised" color="primary"
          style={{'margin': '10px'}}
          onClick={() => this.refs.addDialog.show()}>New Car</Button>
      </div>
    </div>
  );
```

After the modifications, the modal form should look like the following:

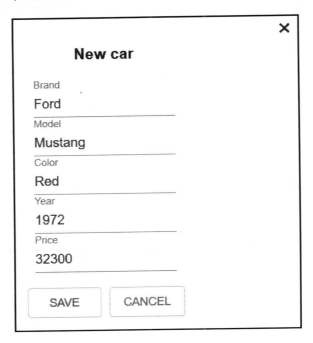

Using the AppBar component

In this section, we'll replace the React app header with an `AppBar` component. Import the `AppBar` and `Toolbar` components:

```
import AppBar from '@material-ui/core/AppBar';
import Toolbar from '@material-ui/core/Toolbar';
```

Remove the `div` header element from the `App.js` file. Add the `AppBar` component to the `render()` method and place the `Toolbar` component inside it. The `Toolbar` component contains the text shown in the app bar:

```
// App.js
import React, { Component } from 'react';
import './App.css';
import Carlist from './components/Carlist';
import AppBar from '@material-ui/core/AppBar';
import Toolbar from '@material-ui/core/Toolbar';
```

```
class App extends Component {
  render() {
    return (
      <div className="App">
        <AppBar position="static" color="default">
          <Toolbar>CarList</ Toolbar>
        </ AppBar>
        <Carlist />
      </div>
    );
  }
}

export default App;
```

Now, your frontend should look like the following:

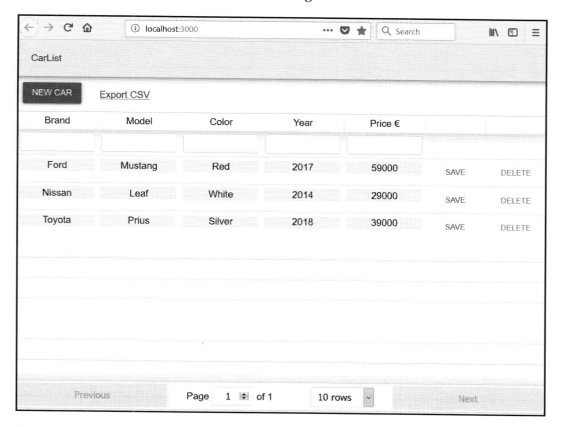

Using the SnackBar component

We have already implemented toast messages by using the `react-toastify` component. Material-UI provides a component, called `SnackBar`, that can be used to show the messages to the end user. To get a uniform outlook in our app, let's use that component for the messages.

We can now remove the `react-toastify` imports from the `Carlist.js` file and we can also remove the component by typing the following command to the terminal you are using:

```
npm remove react-toastify
```

To start using the `Snackbar` component, add the following import to the `Carlist.js` file:

```
import Snackbar from '@material-ui/core/Snackbar';
```

We need two new state values for the `Snackbar`, one for the message and one for the status. Add these two state values to the constructor. The status state is called `open` and it defines whether `Snackbar` is visible or not:

```
constructor(props) {
  super(props);
  this.state = { cars: [], open: false, message: ''};
}
```

Then, we add the `Snackbar` component to the `render()` method. The `autoHideDuration` prop defines the time in milliseconds to wait before `onClose` is called. To show `Snackbar`, we just have to set the `open` state value to `true` and set the message:

```
// Carlist.js render() method's return statement
return (
  <div className="App">
    <Grid container>
      <Grid item>
        <AddCar addCar={this.addCar} fetchCars={this.fetchCars}/>
      </Grid>
      <Grid item style={{padding: 20}}>
        <CSVLink data={this.state.cars} separator=";">Export CSV</CSVLink>
      </Grid>
    </Grid>

    <ReactTable data={this.state.cars} columns={columns}
      filterable={true} pageSize={10}/>
    <Snackbar
      style = {{width: 300, color: 'green'}}
```

```
      open={this.state.open} onClose={this.handleClose}
      autoHideDuration={1500} message={this.state.message} />
  </div>
);
```

Next, we have to implement the `handleClose` function, which is called in the `onClose` event. The function just sets the `open` state value to `false`:

```
handleClose = (event, reason) => {
  this.setState({ open: false });
};
```

Then, we replace the toast messages with the `setState()` methods, which set the `open` value to `true` and the displayed text to the `message` state:

```
// Delete car
onDelClick = (link) => {
  fetch(link, {method: 'DELETE'})
  .then(res => {
    this.setState({open: true, message: 'Car deleted'});
    this.fetchCars();
  })
  .catch(err => {
    this.setState({open: true, message: 'Error when deleting'});
    console.error(err)
  })
}

// Update car
updateCar(car, link) {
  fetch(link,
  { method: 'PUT',
    headers: {
      'Content-Type': 'application/json',
    },
    body: JSON.stringify(car)
  })
  .then( res =>
    this.setState({open: true, message: 'Changes saved'})
  )
  .catch( err =>
    this.setState({open: true, message: 'Error when saving'})
  )
}
```

The following is the screenshot of the message using the `Snackbar` component:

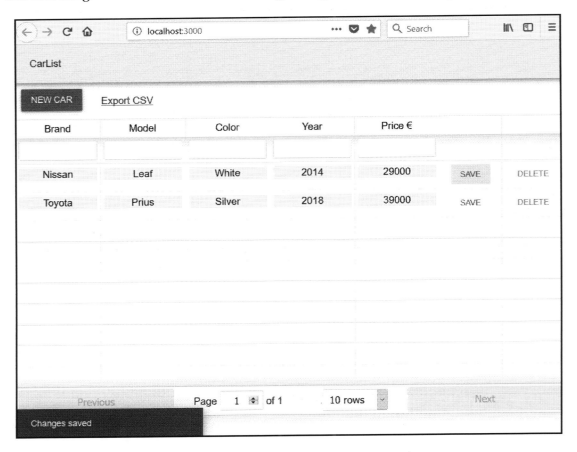

Summary

In this chapter, we finalized our frontend using Material-UI. Material-UI is the React component library that implements Google's Material Design. We replaced all the buttons with the Material-UI `Button` components. Our modal form got a new look by using the Material-UI `TextField` component. We removed the React app header and used the `AppBar` component instead. The messages to the end user are now shown using the `Snackbar` component. After these modifications, our frontend looks more professional and uniform. In the next chapter, we will focus on frontend testing.

Questions

1. What is Material-UI?
2. How should you use different Material-UI components?
3. How should you remove unused components?

Further reading

Packt has other great resources for learning about React:

- https://www.packtpub.com/web-development/getting-started-react
- https://www.packtpub.com/web-development/react-16-essentials-second-edition

12
Testing Your Frontend

This chapter explains the basics of testing React apps. We will give an overview of using Jest, which is a JavaScript test library developed by Facebook. We will also cover Enzyme, which is a testing utility for React, developed by Airbnb. We will look at how you can create new test suites and tests. We will also cover how to run the test and discover the results of the test.

In this chapter, we will look at the following:

- The basics of Jest
- How to create new test suites and tests
- The basics of the Enzyme test utility
- How to install Enzyme
- How to create tests with Enzyme

Technical requirements

The Spring Boot application that we created in Chapter 4, *Securing and Testing Your Backend*, is needed (GitHub: `https://github.com/PacktPublishing/Hands-On-Full-Stack-Development-with-Spring-Boot-2.0-and-React/tree/master/Chapter%204`).

We also need the React app that we used in the previous chapter (GitHub: `https://github.com/PacktPublishing/Hands-On-Full-Stack-Development-with-Spring-Boot-2.0-and-React/tree/master/Chapter%2011`).

Using Jest

Jest is a test library for JavaScript and it is developed by Facebook (`https://facebook.github.io/jest/en/`). Jest is widely used with React and it provides lots of useful features for testing. You can create a snapshot test, where you can take snapshots from React trees and investigate how states are changing. Jest also has mock functionalities that you can use to test, for example, your asynchronous REST API calls. Jest also provides functions that are needed for the assertions in your test cases.

We will first see how you can create a simple test case for a basic JavaScript function, which performs some simple calculations. The following function gets two numbers as arguments and returns the product of the numbers:

```
// multi.js
export const calcMulti = (x, y) => {
    x * y;
}
```

The following code shows a Jest test for the preceding function. The test case starts with a `test` method that runs the test case. The `test` method has an alias, called `it`, and we are using that in the React examples later. The test method gets the two required arguments—the test name and the function that contains the test. `expect` is used when you want to test values. `toBe` is the so-called matcher that checks whether the result from the function equals the value in the matcher. There are many different matchers available in Jest and you can find these from their documentation:

```
// multi.test.js
import {calcMulti} from './multi';

test('2 * 3 equals 6', () => {
  expect(calcMulti(2, 3)).toBe(6);
});
```

Jest comes with `create-react-app`, so we don't have to do any installations or configurations to start testing. It is recommended to create a folder called _test_ for your test files. The test files should have the `.test.js` extension. If you look at your React frontend in the VS Code file explorer, you can see that in the `src` folder, there is already one test file automatically created, and it is called `App.test.js`:

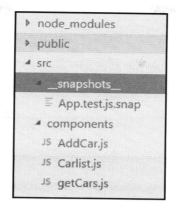

The source code of the test file is as follows:

```
import React from 'react';
import ReactDOM from 'react-dom';
import App from './App';

it('renders without crashing', () => {
  const div = document.createElement('div');
  ReactDOM.render(<App />, div);
  ReactDOM.unmountComponentAtNode(div);
});
```

The following test file creates a div element to the DOM and mounts the App component to it. Finally, the component is unmounted from div. So, it just tests that your App component can be rendered and the test runner is working. it is an alias for the test function in Jest, the first argument is the name of the test, and the second argument is the function that is executed and tested.

You can run your tests by typing the following command into your terminal:

npm test

Or if you are using Yarn, type the following:

yarn test

After your tests have been executed, and everything is working correctly, you will see the following info in the terminal:

```
PASS  src\App.test.js
  √ renders without crashing (156ms)

Test Suites: 1 passed, 1 total
Tests:       1 passed, 1 total
Snapshots:   0 total
Time:        3.623s
Ran all test suites related to changed files.
```

Snapshot testing

Snapshot testing is a useful tool to test that there are no unwanted changes in your user interface. Jest generates snapshot files when the snapshot tests are executed. The next time the tests are executed, the new snapshot is compared to the previous one. If there are changes between the content of the files, the test case fails and an error message is shown in the terminal.

To start snapshot testing, perform the following steps:

1. Install the `react-test-render` package. The `--save-dev` parameter means that this dependency is saved to the `package.json` file's devDependencies part and it is only used for development purposes. If you type the `npm install --production` command in the installation phase, dependencies in the `devDependencies` part are not installed. So, all dependencies that are needed only in the development phase should be installed using the `--save-dev` parameter:

   ```
   npm install react-test-renderer --save-dev
   ```

2. Your `package.json` file should look the following, and the new `devDependecies` part have been added to the file:

   ```
   {
     "name": "carfront",
     "version": "0.1.0",
     "private": true,
     "dependencies": {
       "@material-ui/core": "^1.0.0",
       "@material-ui/icons": "^1.0.0",
       "material-ui": "^0.20.1",
   ```

```
      "react": "^16.3.2",
      "react-confirm-alert": "^2.0.2",
      "react-csv": "^1.0.14",
      "react-dom": "^16.3.2",
      "react-scripts": "1.1.4",
      "react-skylight": "^0.5.1",
      "react-table": "^6.8.2"
    },
    "scripts": {
      "start": "react-scripts start",
      "build": "react-scripts build",
      "test": "react-scripts test --env=jsdom",
      "eject": "react-scripts eject"
    },
    "devDependencies": {
      "react-test-renderer": "^16.3.2"
    }
  }
```

3. Import `renderer` to your test file:

```
import renderer from 'react-test-renderer';
```

Let's add a new snapshot test case to our `App.test.js` file. The test case will create a snapshot test of our `AddCar` component:

1. Import the `AddCar` component to our test file:

```
import AddCar from './components/AddCar';
```

2. Add following test code after the first test case, which already exists in the file. The test case takes a snapshot from our `App` component and then compares whether the snapshot differs from the previous snapshot:

```
it('renders a snapshot', () => {
  const tree = renderer.create(<AddCar/>).toJSON();
  expect(tree).toMatchSnapshot();
});
```

3. Run the test cases again by typing the following command into your terminal:

```
npm test
```

4. Now you can see the following message in the terminal. The test suite tells us the number of test files, and the tests tell us the number of test cases:

```
PASS  src\App.test.js
  √ renders without crashing (148ms)
  √ renders a snapshot (55ms)

Test Suites: 1 passed, 1 total
Tests:       2 passed, 2 total
Snapshots:   1 passed, 1 total
Time:        3.8s, estimated 4s
Ran all test suites related to changed files.
```

When the test is executed for the first time, a _snapshots_ folder is created. This folder contains all the snapshot files that are generated from the test cases. Now, you can see that there is one snapshot file generated, as shown in the following screenshot:

The snapshot file now contains the React tree of our `AddCar` component. You can see part of the snapshot file from the beginning here:

```
// Jest Snapshot v1, https://goo.gl/fbAQLP

exports[`renders a snapshot 1`] = `
<div>
  <section
    className="skylight-wrapper "
  >
    <div
      className="skylight-overlay"
      onClick={[Function]}
      style={
        Object {
          "backgroundColor": "rgba(0,0,0,0.3)",
          "display": "none",
          "height": "100%",
          "left": "0px",
          "position": "fixed",
          "top": "0px",
          "transitionDuration": "200ms",
          "transitionProperty": "all",
          "transitionTimingFunction": "ease",
          "width": "100%",
          "zIndex": "99",
        }
      }
    />
...continue
```

Using Enzyme

Enzyme is a JavaScript library for testing the React component's output and it is developed by Airbnb. Enzyme has a really nice API for DOM manipulation and traversing. If you have used jQuery, it is really easy to understand the idea of the Enzyme API.

To start using Enzyme, perform the following steps:

1. Install it by typing the following command into your terminal. This will install the enzyme library and the adapter library for React version 16. There is an adapter available for older React versions:

```
npm install enzyme enzyme-adapter-react-16 --save-dev
```

2. Create a new test file (test suite) called AddCar.test.js in the src folder. Now we are going to create an Enzyme shallow-rendering test for our AddCar component. The first test case renders the component and checks that there are five TextInput components, as there should be. wrapper.find finds every node in the render tree that matches TextInput. With Enzyme tests, we can use Jest for assertions and here we are using toHaveLength to check that the found node count equals five. Shallow rendering tests the component as a unit and does not render any child components. For this case, shallow rendering is enough. Otherwise you can also use the full DOM rendering by using mount:

```
import React from 'react';
import AddCar from './components/AddCar';
import Enzyme, { shallow } from 'enzyme';
import Adapter from 'enzyme-adapter-react-16';

Enzyme.configure({ adapter: new Adapter() });

describe('<AddCar />', () => {
  it('renders five <TextInput /> components', () => {
    const wrapper = shallow(<AddCar />);
    expect(wrapper.find('TextField')).toHaveLength(5);
  });
});
```

3. Now, if you run the tests, you can see the following message in the terminal. You can also see that the number of test suites is two because the new test file and all tests passed:

```
PASS  src\AddCar.test.js

Test Suites: 2 passed, 2 total
Tests:       3 passed, 3 total
Snapshots:   1 passed, 1 total
Time:        6.212s
Ran all test suites.
```

You can also test events with Enzyme using the `simulate` method. The following example shows how to test the `onChange` event of the `TextField` brand in the `AddCar` component. This example also shows how to access the state of the component. We first use `wrapper.find` to find the first `TextField`, which is used for the car brand. Then, we set the value of `TextField` and use the `simulate` method to simulate the change event. Finally, we check the value of the brand state that should now contain `Ford`:

```
describe('<AddCar />', () => {
  it('test onChange', () => {
    const wrapper = shallow(<AddCar />);
    const brandInput = wrapper.find('TextField').get(0);
    brandInput.instance().value = 'Ford';
    usernameInput.simulate('change');
    expect(wrapper.state('brand')).toEqual('Ford');
  });
});
```

Summary

In this chapter, we gave a basic overview of how to test React apps. Jest is a testing library developed by Facebook, and it is already available in our frontend because we created our app with `create-react-app`. We created a couple of tests with Jest, and ran those tests to see how you can check the results of tests. We installed Enzyme, which is a test utility for React. With Enzyme, you can easily test your React component rendering and events. In the next chapter, we will secure our application, and add the login functionality to the frontend.

Questions

1. What is Jest?
2. How should you create test cases using Jest?
3. How should you create a snapshot test using Jest?
4. What is Enzyme?
5. How should you install Enzyme?
6. How should you test rendering with Enzyme?
7. How should you test events with Enzyme?

Further reading

Packt has other great resources for learning about React and testing:

- `https://www.packtpub.com/web-development/react-16-tooling`
- `https://www.packtpub.com/web-development/jasmine-javascript-testing-second-edition`

Securing Your Application 13

This chapter explains how to implement authentication to our frontend when we are using JWT authentication in the backend. At the beginning, we switch on security to our backend to enable JWT authentication. Then, we create a component for the login functionality. Finally, we modify our CRUD functionalities to send the token in the request's `Authorization` header to the backend.

In this chapter, we will look at the following:

- How to create a login functionality on our frontend
- How to implement conditional rendering after authentication
- What is needed for CRUD functionalities when the JWT authentication is enabled
- How to show messages when authentication fails

Technical requirements

The Spring Boot application that we created in `Chapter 4`, *Securing and Testing Your Backend*, (GitHub: `https://github.com/PacktPublishing/Hands-On-Full-Stack-Development-with-Spring-Boot-2.0-and-React/tree/master/Chapter%204`).

The React app that we used in the previous chapter (GitHub: `https://github.com/PacktPublishing/Hands-On-Full-Stack-Development-with-Spring-Boot-2.0-and-React/tree/master/Chapter%2011`).

Securing the backend

We have implemented CRUD functionalities to our frontend using an unsecured backend. Now, it is time to switch on security again for our backend and go back to the version that we created in Chapter 4, *Securing and Testing Your Backend*:

1. Open your backend project with the Eclipse IDE and open the
   `SecurityConfig.java` file in the editor view. We commented the security out and allowed everyone access to all endpoints. Now, we can remove that line and also remove the comments from the original version. Now your
   `SecurityConfig.java` file's `configure` method should look like the following:

```
@Override
  protected void configure(HttpSecurity http) throws Exception {
    http.csrf().disable().cors().and().authorizeRequests()
    .antMatchers(HttpMethod.POST, "/login").permitAll()
    .anyRequest().authenticated()
    .and()
    // Filter for the api/login requests
    .addFilterBefore(new LoginFilter("/login",
authenticationManager()),
        UsernamePasswordAuthenticationFilter.class)
    // Filter for other requests to check JWT in header
    .addFilterBefore(new AuthenticationFilter(),
        UsernamePasswordAuthenticationFilter.class);
  }
```

Let's test what happens when the backend is now secured again.

2. Run the backend by pressing the **Run** button in Eclipse and check from the **Console** view that the application started correctly. Run the frontend by typing the `npm start` command into your terminal and the browser should be opened to the address `localhost:3000`.

3. You should now see the list page and the table are empty. If you open the developer tools, you will notice that the request ends in the `403 Forbidden` HTTP error. This is actually what we wanted because we haven't done the authentication yet to our frontend:

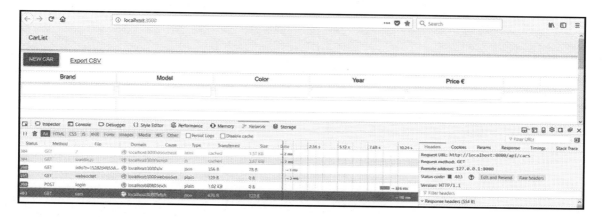

Securing the frontend

The authentication was implemented to the backend using JWT. In `Chapter 4`, *Securing and Testing Your Backend,* we created JWT authentication, and the `/login` endpoint is allowed to everyone without authentication. In the frontend's login page we have to first call `/login` endpoint to get the token. After that, the token will be included to all requests we are sending to the backend, as was demonstrated in `Chapter 4`, *Securing and Testing Your Backend.*

Let's first create a login component that asks for credentials from the user to get a token from the backend:

1. Create a new file, called `Login.js`, in the `components` folder. Now, your file structure of the frontend should be the following:

2. Open the file in the VS Code editor view and add the following base code to the login component. We are also importing `SERVER_URL` because it is needed in a login request:

```
import React, { Component } from 'react';
import {SERVER_URL} from '../constants.js';

class Login extends Component {
  render() {
    return (
      <div>
      </div>
    );
```

```
  }
}

export default Login;
```

3. We need three state values for authentication. Two for the credentials (`username` and `password`) and one Boolean value to indicate the status of authentication. The default value of the authentication status state is `false`. Create the `constructor` and introduce states inside the `constructor`:

```
constructor(props) {
  super(props);
  this.state = {username: '', password: '',
    isAuthenticated: false};
}
```

4. In the user interface, we are going to use the Material-UI component library, as we did with the rest of the user interface. We need text field components for the credentials and a button to call a login function. Add imports for the components to the `login.js` file:

```
import TextField from '@material-ui/core/TextField';
import Button from '@material-ui/core/Button';
```

5. Add imported components to a user interface by adding these to the `render()` method. We need two `TextField` components, one for the username and one for the password. One `RaisedButton` component is needed to call the `login` function that we are going to implement later in this section:

```
render() {
  return (
    <div>
      <TextField name="username" placeholder="Username"
      onChange={this.handleChange} /><br/>
      <TextField type="password" name="password"
       placeholder="Password"
      onChange={this.handleChange} /><br/><br/>
      <Button variant="raised" color="primary"
       onClick={this.login}>
        Login
      </Button>
    </div>
  );
}
```

6. Implement the change handler for the `TextField` components to save typed values to the states:

```
handleChange = (event) => {
  this.setState({[event.target.name] : event.target.value});
}
```

7. As shown in `Chapter 4`, *Securing and Testing Your Backend*, the login is done by calling the `/login` endpoint using the `POST` method and sending the user object inside the body. If authentication succeeds, we get a token in a response `Authorization` header. We will then save the token to session storage and set the `isAuthenticated` state value to `true`. The session storage is similar to local storage but it is cleared when a page session ends. When the `isAuthenticated` state value is changed, the user interface is re-rendered:

```
login = () => {
  const user = {username: this.state.username, password:
this.state.password};
  fetch(SERVER_URL + 'login', {
    method: 'POST',
    body: JSON.stringify(user)
  })
  .then(res => {
    const jwtToken = res.headers.get('Authorization');
    if (jwtToken !== null) {
      sessionStorage.setItem("jwt", jwtToken);
      this.setState({isAuthenticated: true});
    }
  })
  .catch(err => console.error(err))
}
```

8. We can implement conditional rendering, which renders the `Login` component if the `isAuthenticated` state is `false` or the `Carlist` component if `isAuthenticated` state is `true`. We first have to import the `Carlist` component to the `Login` component:

```
import Carlist from './Carlist';
```

And then implement the following changes to the `render()` method:

```
render() {
  if (this.state.isAuthenticated === true) {
    return (<Carlist />)
  }
  else {
    return (
      <div>
        <TextField type="text" name="username"
         placeholder="Username"
        onChange={this.handleChange} /><br/>
        <TextField type="password" name="password"
         placeholder="Password"
        onChange={this.handleChange} /><br/><br/>
        <Button variant="raised" color="primary"
         onClick={this.login}>
          Login
        </Button>
      </div>
    );
  }
}
```

9. To show the login form, we have to render the `Login` component instead of the `Carlist` component in the `App.js` file:

```
// App.js
import React, { Component } from 'react';
import './App.css';
import Login from './components/Login';
import AppBar from '@material-ui/core/AppBar';
import Toolbar from '@material-ui/core/Toolbar';

class App extends Component {
  render() {
    return (
      <div className="App">
        <AppBar position="static" color="default">
          <Toolbar>CarList</ Toolbar>
        </ AppBar>
        <Login />
      </div>
    );
  }
```

```
    }

    export default App;
```

Now, when your frontend and backend are running, your frontend should look like the following:

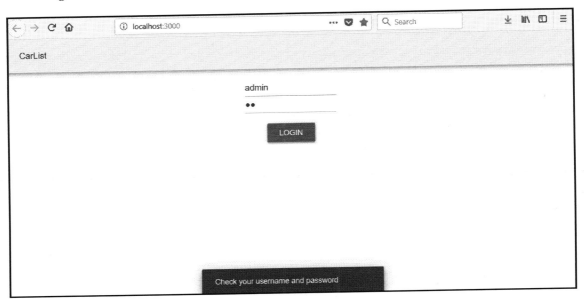

And if you log in using the `user/user` or `admin/admin` credentials, you should see the car list page. If you open the developer tools, you can see that the token is now saved to session storage:

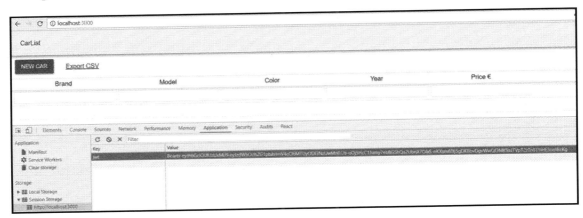

The car list is still empty, but that is correct because we haven't included the token to the request yet. That is needed for JWT authentication, which we will implement in the next phase:

1. Open the `Carlist.js` file in the VS Code editor view. To fetch the cars, we first have to read the token from the session storage and then add the `Authorization` header with the token value to the request. You can see the source code of the fetch function here:

```
// Carlist.js
// Fetch all cars
fetchCars = () => {
  // Read the token from the session storage
  // and include it to Authorization header
  const token = sessionStorage.getItem("jwt");
  fetch(SERVER_URL + 'api/cars',
  {
    headers: {'Authorization': token}
  })
  .then((response) => response.json())
  .then((responseData) => {
    this.setState({
      cars: responseData._embedded.cars,
    });
  })
  .catch(err => console.error(err));
}
```

2. If you log in to your frontend, you should see the car list populated with cars from the database:

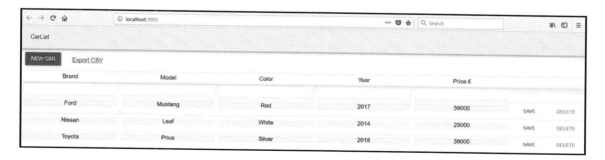

3. Check the request content from the developer tools; you can see that it contains the `Authorization` header with the token value:

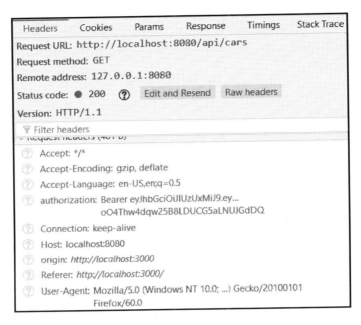

All other CRUD functionalities need the same modification to work correctly. The source code of the delete function looks like the following, after the modifications:

```
// Delete car
onDelClick = (link) => {
  const token = sessionStorage.getItem("jwt");
  fetch(link,
    {
      method: 'DELETE',
      headers: {'Authorization': token}
    }
  )
  .then(res => {
    this.setState({open: true, message: 'Car deleted'});
    this.fetchCars();
  })
  .catch(err => {
    this.setState({open: true, message: 'Error when deleting'});
    console.error(err)
  })
}
```

The source code of the add function looks as follows, after the modifications:

```
// Add new car
addCar(car) {
  const token = sessionStorage.getItem("jwt");
  fetch(SERVER_URL + 'api/cars',
  { method: 'POST',
      headers: {
        'Content-Type': 'application/json',
        'Authorization': token
      },
      body: JSON.stringify(car)
  })
  .then(res => this.fetchCars())
  .catch(err => console.error(err))
}
```

And finally, the source code of the update function looks like this:

```
// Update car
updateCar(car, link) {
  const token = sessionStorage.getItem("jwt");
  fetch(link,
  { method: 'PUT',
    headers: {
      'Content-Type': 'application/json',
      'Authorization': token
    },
    body: JSON.stringify(car)
  })
  .then( res =>
    this.setState({open: true, message: 'Changes saved'})
  )
  .catch( err =>
    this.setState({open: true, message: 'Error when saving'})
  )
}
```

Now, all the CRUD functionalities are working after you have logged in to the application.

In the final phase, we are going to implement an error message that is shown to an end user if authentication fails. We are using the Material-UI `SnackBar` component to show the message:

1. Add the following import to the `Login.js` file:

```
import Snackbar from '@material-ui/core/Snackbar';
```

2. Open the state for Snackbar, as we did in Chapter 10, *Adding CRUD Functionalities*:

```
// Login.js
constructor(props) {
  super(props);
  this.state = {username: '', password: '',
  isAuthenticated: false, open: false};
}
```

We also need a state handler for the `Snackbar` open state to close `Snackbar` after the time that we set in the `Snackbar` `autoHideDuration` props:

```
handleClose = (event) => {
  this.setState({ open: false });
}
```

3. Add `Snackbar` to the `render()` method:

```
<Snackbar
  open={this.state.open} onClose={this.handleClose}
  autoHideDuration={1500}
  message='Check your username and password' />
```

4. Set the `open` state value to `true` if the authentication fails:

```
login = () => {
  const user = {username: this.state.username,
      password: this.state.password};
  fetch('http://localhost:8080/login', {
    method: 'POST',
    body: JSON.stringify(user)
  })
  .then(res => {
    const jwtToken = res.headers.get('Authorization');
    if (jwtToken !== null) {
      sessionStorage.setItem("jwt", jwtToken);
      this.setState({isAuthenticated: true});
    }
```

```
      else {
        this.setState({open: true});
      }
    })
    .catch(err => console.error(err))
}
```

If you now log in with the wrong credentials, you can see the toast message:

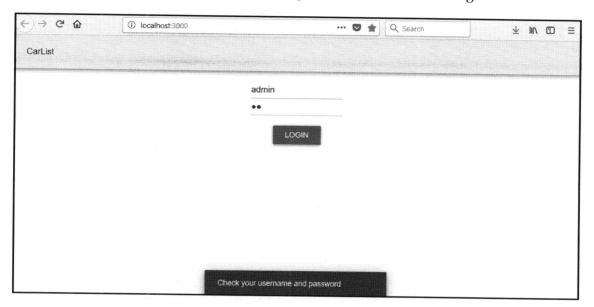

The logout functionality is much more straightforward to implement. You basically just have to remove the token from session storage and change the isAuthenticated state value to false, as shown in the following source code:

```
logout = () => {
    sessionStorage.removeItem("jwt");
    this.setState({isAuthenticated: false});
}
```

Then with conditional rendering, you can render the Login component instead of Carlist.

If you want to implement a menu using React Router, it is possible to implement so-called secured routes that can be accessed only when a user is authenticated. The following source code shows the secured route that shows the routed component if the user is authenticated, otherwise it redirects to a login page:

```
const SecuredRoute = ({ component: Component, ...rest, isAuthenticated })
=> (
  <Route {...rest} render={props => (
    isAuthenticated ? (
      <Component {...props}/>
    ) : (
      <Redirect to={{
        pathname: '/login',
        state: { from: props.location }
      }}/>
    )
  )}/>
)
```

Here is the example of the `Switch` router that is using `SecuredRoute`, which we defined in the previous example. The `Login` and `Contact` components can be accessed without authentication, but `Shop` needs authentication:

```
<Switch>
   <Route path="/login" component={Login} />
   <Route path="/contact" component={Contact} />
   <SecuredRoute isAuthenticated={this.state.isAuthenticated}
     path="/shop" component={Shop} />
   <Route render={() => <h1>Page not found</h1>} />
</Switch>
```

Summary

In this chapter, we learned how to implement a login functionality for our frontend when we are using JWT authentication. After successful authentication, we used session storage to save the token that we received from the backend. The token was then used in all requests that we sent to the backend, therefore, we had to modify our CRUD functionalities to work properly with authentication. In the next chapter, we will deploy our application to Heroku and we demonstrate how to create Docker containers.

Questions

1. How should you create a login form?
2. How should you log in to the backend using JWT?
3. How should you store tokens to session storage?
4. How should you send a token to the backend in CRUD functions?

Further reading

Packt has other great resources for learning about React:

- https://www.packtpub.com/web-development/react-16-tooling
- https://www.packtpub.com/web-development/react-16-essentials-second-edition

Deploying Your Application **14**

This chapter explains how to deploy your backend and frontend to a server. There are a variety of cloud servers or **PaaS (Platform as a Service)** providers available, such as Amazon (AWS), DigitalOcean, and Microsoft Azure. In this book, we are using Heroku, which supports multiple programming languages that are used in web development. We will also show you how to use Docker containers in deployment.

In this chapter, we will look at the following:

- Different options for deploying the Spring Boot application
- How to deploy the Spring Boot application to Heroku
- How to deploy the React app to Heroku
- How to create the Spring Boot and MariaDB Docker container

Technical requirements

The Spring Boot application that we created in `Chapter 4`, *Securing and Testing Your Backend*, is required (GitHub: `https://github.com/PacktPublishing/Hands-On-Full-Stack-Development-with-Spring-Boot-2.0-and-React/tree/master/Chapter%204`).

The React app that we used in the previous chapter is also required (GitHub: `https://github.com/PacktPublishing/Hands-On-Full-Stack-Development-with-Spring-Boot-2.0-and-React/tree/master/Chapter%2011`).

Docker installation is necessary.

Deploying the backend

If you are going to use your own server, the easiest way to deploy the Spring Boot application is to use an executable JAR file. An executable JAR file is generated, if you use Maven, in the command line by typing the mvn clean install command. That command creates the JAR file in the build folder. In this case, you don't have to install a separate application server because it is embedded in your JAR file. Then you just have to run the JAR file using the java command, java -jar your_appfile.jar. The embedded Tomcat version can be defined in the pom.xml file with the following lines:

```
<properties>
   <tomcat.version>8.0.52</tomcat.version>
</properties>
```

If you are using a separate application server, you have to create a WAR package. That is a little bit more complicated and you have to make some modifications to your application. The following are the steps to create the WAR file:

1. Modify an application main class by extending SpringBootServletIntializer and overriding the configure method:

```
@SpringBootApplication
public class Application extends SpringBootServletInitializer {
    @Override
    protected SpringApplicationBuilder configure
        (SpringApplicationBuilder application) {
        return application.sources(Application.class);
    }

    public static void main(String[] args) throws Exception {
        SpringApplication.run(Application.class, args);
    }
}
```

2. Change the packaging from JAR to WAR in the pom.xml file:

```
<packaging>war</packaging>
```

3. Add the following dependency to the `pom.xml` file. Then, the Tomcat application is no longer embedded:

```
<dependency>
    <groupId>org.springframework.boot</groupId>
    <artifactId>spring-boot-starter-tomcat</artifactId>
    <scope>provided</scope>
</dependency>
```

Now, when you build your application, the WAR file is generated. It can be deployed to the existing Tomcat by copying the file to Tomcat's `/webapps` folder.

Nowadays, cloud servers are the major way to provide your application to end users. Next, we are going to deploy our backend to the Heroku cloud server (`https://www.heroku.com/`). Heroku offers a free account that you can use to deploy your own applications. With the free account, your applications go to sleep after 30 minutes of inactivity and it takes a little bit more time to restart application. But the free account is enough for testing and hobby purposes.

For deployment, you can use Heroku's web-based user interface. The following steps go through the deployment process:

1. After you have created an account with Heroku, log in to the Heroku website. Navigate to the dashboard that shows a list of your applications. There is a button called **New** that opens a menu. Select **Create new app** from the menu:

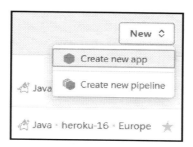

2. Name your app, select a region, and press the **Create app** button:

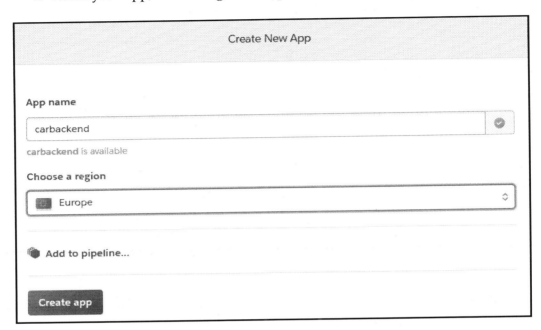

3. Select a deployment method. There are several options; we are using the **GitHub** option. In that method, you first have to push your application to GitHub and then link your GitHub repository to Heroku:

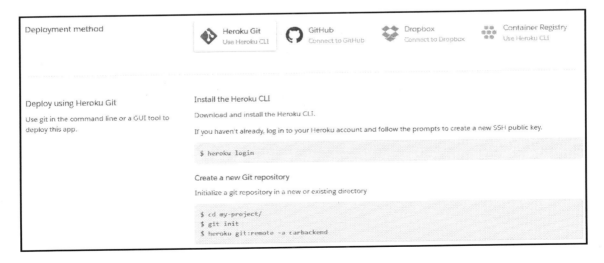

4. Search for a repository you want to deploy to and then press the **Connect** button:

5. Choose between automatic and manual deployment. The automatic option deploys your app automatically when you push a new version to connected the GitHub repository. You also have to select a branch you want to deploy. We will now use the manual option that deploys the app when you press the **Deploy branch** button:

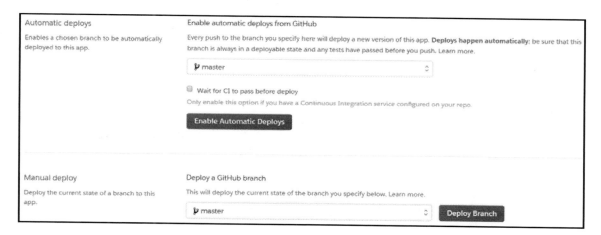

6. Deployment starts and you can see a build log. You should see a message that says **Your app was successfully deployed**:

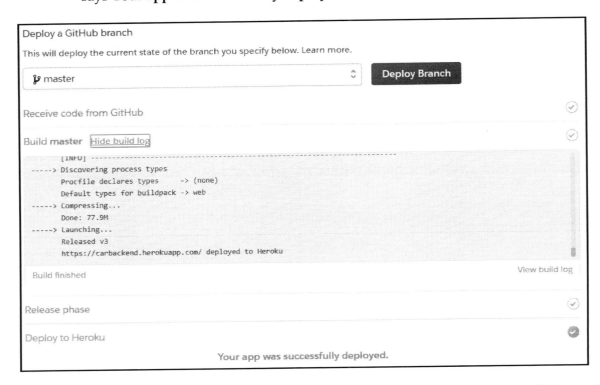

Now, your application is deployed to the Heroku cloud server. If you are using the H2 in-memory database, this would be enough and your application should work. We are using MariaDB; therefore, we have to install the database.

In Heroku, we can use JawsDB, which is available in Heroku as an add-on. JawsDB is a **Database as a Service (DBaaS)** provider that offers MariaDB database, which can be used in Heroku. The following steps describe how to start using the database:

1. Open a **Resources** tab in your Heroku app page and type JawsDB into the **Add-ons** search field:

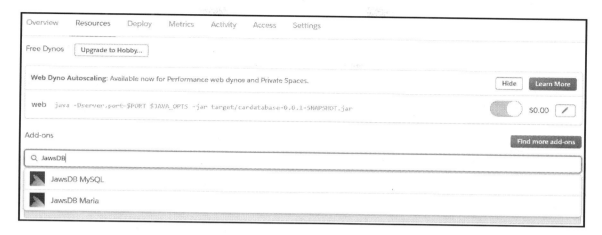

2. Select **JawsDB Maria** from the dropdown list. You can see JawsDB in your adds-on list. Click **JawsDB** and you can see the connection info of your database:

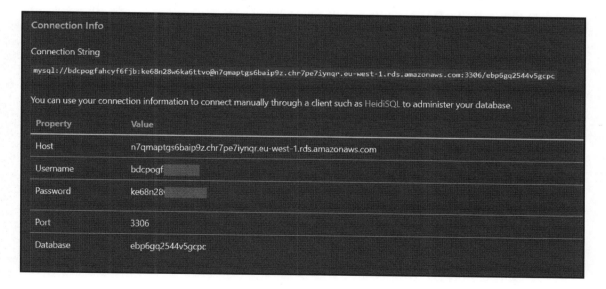

3. Change the database connection definition in the `application.properties` file with the values from the JawsDB connection info page. In this example we use plain password but it is recommended to encrypt password using for example, **Java Simplified Encryption (JASYPT)** library:

```
spring.datasource.url=jdbc:mariadb://n7qmaptgs6baip9z.chr7pe7iynqr.
eu-west-1.rds.amazonaws.com:3306/ebp6gq2544v5gcpc
spring.datasource.username=bdcpogfxxxxxxx
spring.datasource.password=ke68n28xxxxxxx
spring.datasource.driver-class-name=org.mariadb.jdbc.Driver
```

4. With the free account, we can have a maximum of 10 concurrent connections to our database; therefore, we also have to add the following line to the `application.properties` file:

```
spring.datasource.max-active=10
```

5. Push your changes to GitHub and deploy your app in Heroku. Now, your application is ready and we can test that with Postman. The URL of the app is `https://carbackend.herokuapp.com/`, but you can also use your own domain. If we send the POST request to the `/login` endpoint with the credential, we can get the token in the response header. So, everything seems to work properly:

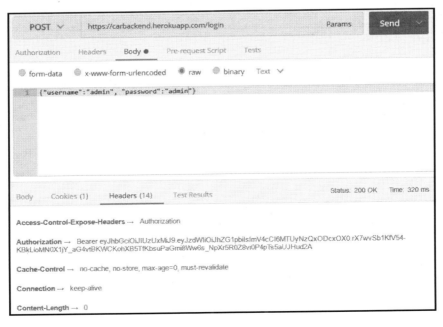

You can also connect to the JawsDB database with HeidiSQL, and we can see that our car database has been created:

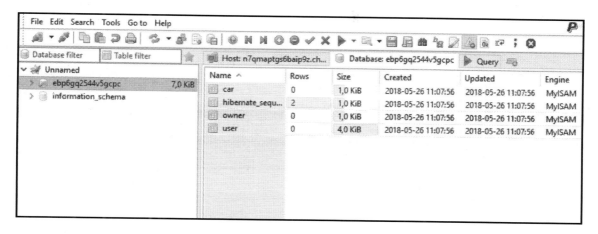

You can watch application logs by selecting **View logs** from the **More** menu:

The application log view looks like the following.

Deploying the frontend

In this section, we will deploy our React frontend to Heroku. The easiest way to deploy the React app to Heroku is to use the Heroku Buildpack for create-react-app (`https://github.com/mars/create-react-app-buildpack`). For deployment, we have to install the Heroku CLI, which is the command-line tool for Heroku. You can download the installation package from `https://devcenter.heroku.com/articles/heroku-cli`. After the installation has finished, you can use the Heroku CLI from PowerShell or the Terminal you're using. The following steps describe the deployment process:

1. Open your frontend project with VS Code and open the `constant.js` file in the editor. Change the `SERVER_URL` constant to match our backend's URL and save the changes:

   ```
   export const SERVER_URL = 'https://carbackend.herokuapp.com/'
   ```

2. Create a local Git repository to your project and commit the files, if you haven't done that, yet. Navigate to your project folder with the Git command-line tool and type the following commands:

   ```
   git init
   git add .
   git commit —m "Heroku deployment"
   ```

3. The following command creates a new Heroku app and asks for credentials to log in to Heroku. Replace [APPNAME] with your own app name. After the command has been executed, you should see the new app in your Heroku dashboard:

```
heroku create [APPNAME] --buildpack
https://github.com/mars/create-react-app-buildpack.git
```

4. Deploy your code to Heroku by typing the following command to PowerShell:

```
git push heroku master
```

After the deployment is ready, you should see the **Verifying deploy... done** message in PowerShell, as shown in the following screenshot:

```
remote:
remote: The build folder is ready to be deployed.
remote: You may serve it with a static server:
remote:
remote:   yarn global add serve
remote:   serve -s build
remote:
remote: Find out more about deployment here:
remote:
remote:   http://bit.ly/2vY88Kr
remote:
remote: =====> Downloading Buildpack: https://github.com/heroku/heroku-buildpack-static.git
remote: =====> Detected Framework: Static HTML
remote:    % Total    % Received % Xferd  Average Speed   Time    Time     Time  Current
remote:                                   Dload  Upload   Total   Spent    Left  Speed
remote: 100  838k  100  838k    0     0  5894k      0 --:--:-- --:--:-- --:--:-- 5905k
remote: -----> Installed directory to /app/bin
remote: Using release configuration from last framework (Static HTML).
remote: -----> Discovering process types
remote:        Procfile declares types      -> (none)
remote:        Default types for buildpack -> web
remote:
remote: -----> Compressing...
remote:        Done: 47.6M
remote: -----> Launching...
remote:        Released v4
remote:        https://carfront.herokuapp.com/ deployed to Heroku
remote:
remote: Verifying deploy... done.
To https://git.heroku.com/carfront.git
   32a5ecd..4565486  master -> master
```

Now, you can go to your Heroku dashboard and see the URL of your frontend; you can also open it from the Heroku CLI by typing the `heroku open` command. If you navigate to your frontend, you should see the login form:

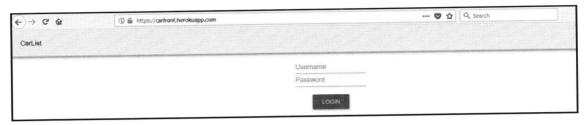

Using Docker containers

Docker is a container platform that makes software development, deployment, and shipping easier. Containers are lightweight and executable software packages that include everything that is needed to run software. In this section, we are creating a container from our Spring Boot backend, as follows:

1. Install Docker to your workstation. You can find the installation packages at `https://www.docker.com/get-docker`. There are installation packages for multiple platforms and if you have Windows operating system, you can go through the installation wizard using the default settings.
2. The Spring Boot application is just an executable JAR file that can be executed with Java. The JAR file can be created with the following Maven command:

```
mvn clean install
```

You can also use Eclipse to run Maven goals by opening the **Run | Run configurations...** menu. Select your project in the **Base directory** field, using the **Workspace** button. Type **clean install** into the **Goals** field and press the **Run** button:

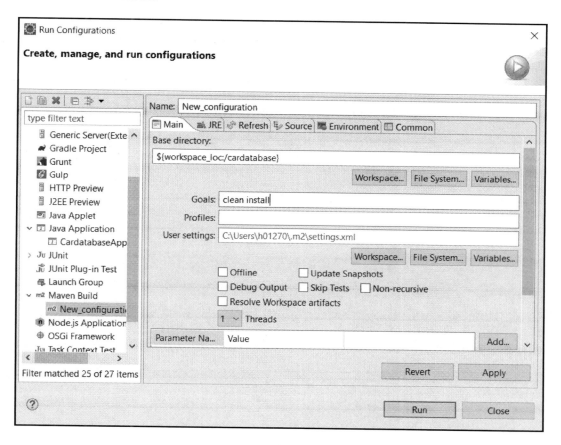

3. After the build is finished, you can find the executable JAR file from the `/target` folder:

classes	27.5.2018 13:09	File folder	
generated-sources	27.5.2018 13:09	File folder	
generated-test-sources	27.5.2018 13:09	File folder	
maven-archiver	27.5.2018 13:09	File folder	
maven-status	27.5.2018 13:09	File folder	
surefire-reports	27.5.2018 13:09	File folder	
test-classes	27.5.2018 13:09	File folder	
cardatabase-0.0.1-SNAPSHOT.jar	27.5.2018 13:09	Executable Jar File	31 380 KB
cardatabase-0.0.1-SNAPSHOT.jar.original	27.5.2018 13:09	ORIGINAL File	17 KB

4. You can test that the build went correctly by running the JAR file with the following command:

```
java -jar .\cardatabase-0.0.1-SNAPSHOT.jar
```

5. You'll see the application's starting messages and, finally, your application is running:

Containers are defined by using Dockerfiles.

6. Create a new Dockerfile in the root folder of your project and name it
   `Dockerfile`. The following lines show the content of the Dockerfile. We are
   using Alpine Linux. `EXPOSE` defines the port that should be published outside of
   the container. `COPY` copies the JAR file to the container's filesystem and renames
   it `app.jar`. `ENTRYPOINT` defines the command-line arguments that the Docker
   container runs.

There is also a Maven plugin available to build Docker images. It is
developed by Spotify and can be found at `https://github.com/spotify/`
`docker-maven-plugin`.

The following lines show the content of `Dockerfile`.

```
FROM openjdk:8-jdk-alpine
VOLUME /tmp
EXPOSE 8080
ARG JAR_FILE
COPY target/cardatabase-0.0.1-SNAPSHOT.jar app.jar
ENTRYPOINT ["java","-Djava.security.egd=file:/dev/./urandom","-
jar","/app.jar"]
```

7. Create the container with the following command. With the $-t$ argument, we can
   give a friendly name to our container:

```
docker build -t carbackend .
```

At the end of the build command, you should see the **Successfully built** message:

```
PS C:\work\carBackEnd> docker build -t carbackend .
Sending build context to Docker daemon  32.67MB
Step 1/5 : FROM openjdk:8-jdk-alpine
 ---> 224765a6bdbe
Step 2/5 : VOLUME /tmp
 ---> Using cache
 ---> a03de6ca0e4e
Step 3/5 : ARG JAR_FILE
 ---> Using cache
 ---> f237684c815f
Step 4/5 : COPY target/cardatabase-0.0.1-SNAPSHOT.jar app.jar
 ---> Using cache
 ---> 13c0ee6b4cd2
Step 5/5 : ENTRYPOINT ["java","-Djava.security.egd=file:/dev/./urandom","-jar","/app.jar"]
 ---> Using cache
 ---> 7edc33ec6be6
Successfully built 7edc33ec6be6
Successfully tagged carbackend:latest
```

8. Check the list of the container using the `docker image ls` command:

```
PS C:\work\carBackEnd> docker image ls
REPOSITORY        TAG            IMAGE ID          CREATED          SIZE
carbackend        latest         7edc33ec6be6      2 minutes ago    134MB
openjdk           8-jdk-alpine   224765a6bdbe      4 months ago     102MB
```

9. Run the container with the following command:

```
docker run -p 4000:8080 carbackend
```

The Spring Boot application starts but it ends with an error because we are trying to access the localhost database. The localhost now points to the container itself and there is no MariaDB installed.

10. We will create our own container for MariaDB. You can pull the latest MariaDB container from the Docker Hub using the following command:

```
docker pull mariadb:lates
```

11. Run the MariaDB container. The following command sets the root user password and creates a new database, called `cardb`, that we need for our Spring Boot application:

```
docker run --name cardb -e MYSQL_ROOT_PASSWORD=pwd -e
MYSQL_DATABASE=cardb mariadb
```

12. We have to make one change to our Spring Boot `application.properties` file. Change the `datasource` URL to the following. In the next step, we will specify that our application can access the database container using the `mariadb` name. After the change, you have to build your application and re-create the Spring Boot container:

```
spring.datasource.url=jdbc:mariadb://mariadb:3306/cardb
```

13. We can run our Spring Boot container and link the MariaDB container to it using the following command. The command now defines that our Spring Boot container can access the MariaDB container using the `mariadb` name:

```
docker run -p 8080:8080 --name carapp --link cardb:mariadb -d
carbackend
```

14. We can also access our application logs by typing the `docker logs carapp` command. We can see that our application has started successfully and the demo data has been inserted into the database that exists in the MariaDB container:

```
s): 8080 (http) with context path ''
2018-05-27 12:48:34.234  INFO 1 --- [           main] c.p.cardatabase.CardatabaseApplication   : Started CardatabaseAppl
ication in 6.67 seconds (JVM running for 7.3)
Hibernate: select next_val as id_val from hibernate_sequence for update
Hibernate: update hibernate_sequence set next_val= ? where next_val=?
Hibernate: insert into owner (firstname, lastname, ownerid) values (?, ?, ?)
Hibernate: select next_val as id_val from hibernate_sequence for update
Hibernate: update hibernate_sequence set next_val= ? where next_val=?
Hibernate: insert into owner (firstname, lastname, ownerid) values (?, ?, ?)
Hibernate: select next_val as id_val from hibernate_sequence for update
Hibernate: update hibernate_sequence set next_val= ? where next_val=?
Hibernate: insert into car (brand, color, model, owner, price, register_number, year, id) values (?, ?, ?, ?, ?, ?, ?, ?
)
Hibernate: select next_val as id_val from hibernate_sequence for update
Hibernate: update hibernate_sequence set next_val= ? where next_val=?
Hibernate: insert into car (brand, color, model, owner, price, register_number, year, id) values (?, ?, ?, ?, ?, ?, ?, ?
)
Hibernate: select next_val as id_val from hibernate_sequence for update
Hibernate: update hibernate_sequence set next_val= ? where next_val=?
Hibernate: insert into car (brand, color, model, owner, price, register_number, year, id) values (?, ?, ?, ?, ?, ?, ?, ?
)
Hibernate: insert into user (password, role, username) values (?, ?, ?)
Hibernate: insert into user (password, role, username) values (?, ?, ?)
```

Summary

In this chapter, we learned how to deploy the Spring Boot application. We went through the different deployment options of the Spring Boot application and deployed the application to Heroku. Next, we deployed our React frontend to Heroku using the Heroku Buildpack for create-react-app, which makes the deployment process fast. Finally, we used Docker to create containers from our Spring Boot application and MariaDB database. In the next chapter, we will cover some more technologies and best practises that you should explore.

Questions

1. How should you create a Spring Boot-executable JAR file?
2. How should you deploy the Spring Boot application to Heroku?
3. How should you deploy the React app to Heroku?
4. What is Docker?
5. How should you create the Spring Boot application container?
6. How should you create the MariaDB container?

Further reading

Packt has other great resources for learning about React, Spring Boot, and Docker:

- `https://www.packtpub.com/web-development/react-16-tooling`
- `https://www.packtpub.com/web-development/react-16-essentials-second-edition`
- `https://www.packtpub.com/virtualization-and-cloud/deployment-docker`
- `https://www.packtpub.com/virtualization-and-cloud/docker-fundamentals-integrated-course`

15
Best Practices

This chapter goes through some points that you should know if you want to become a full stack developer or if you want progress further in your software-development career. We will also go through some best practices that are good to keep in mind when you're working in the field of software development.

In this chapter, we will look at the following:

- What kind of technologies you should know
- What kind of best practices are important to you

What to learn next

To become a full stack developer, you have to be able to work with both the backend and the frontend. That sounds like quite a challenging task, but if you focus on the right things and don't try to master everything, it is possible. Nowadays, the technology stack available is huge and you might often wonder what you should learn next. There are multiple factors that might give you some hints about where to go next. One way is to browse job opportunities and see which technologies companies are looking for.

There are multiple ways, and no right path, to start learning a new technology. The usage of programming web courses is a really popular starting point and that gives you basic knowledge to start the learning process. The process is never-ending because technologies are developing and changing all the time.

The following technologies are necessary to understand if you want to become a full stack developer. This is not the complete list, but it is a good starting point.

HTML

HTML is the most fundamental thing in web development that you should learn. You don't have to master all the details of HTML, but you should have a good basic knowledge of it. HTML 5 introduced a lot of new features that are also worth learning.

CSS

CSS is also a very basic thing to learn. The good thing is that there are lots of good tutorials available for both HTML and CSS. It is a good idea also to learn the usage of some CSS libraries, such as Bootstrap, which is widely used. CSS preprocessors, such as SASS and LESS, are also worth learning.

HTTP

HTTP protocol is the key part when developing web applications and RESTful Web Services. You have to understand the basics of HTTP and know its limitations. You should also know what kind of methods exist and how to use these with different programming languages.

JavaScript

JavaScript is definitely the programming language that you should master. Without JavaScript skills, it is really hard to work with a modern frontend development. ES6 is also good to learn because that makes JavaScript coding cleaner and more efficient.

A backend programming language

It's hard to survive without knowing a few programming languages. If JavaScript is used for frontend development, it can also be used in the backend with Node.js. That is the benefit with Node.js; you can use one programming language in the frontend and the backend. Other popular languages for backend development are Java, C#, Python, and PHP. All these languages also have good backend frameworks you can use.

Some frontend libraries or frameworks

In this book, we used React.js in the frontend, which is currently a popular option, but there are many others that are also good options, such as Angular and Vue.js.

Databases

You should also know how to use databases with your backend programming language. The database can be either a SQL or NoSQL database, and it is good to know both options. You should also know how performance can be optimized with the database you are using and the queries you are executing.

Version control

The version control is something that you can't live without. Nowadays, Git is a really popular version control system and it's really important to know how to use it. There are also repository management services, such as GitHub and GitLab, that are good to know.

Useful tools

There are also many different tools that can help to make your development process more efficient. Here, we just mention some tools that might be useful for you. Gulp.js is an open source JavaScript toolkit to automate your tasks in the development process. Grunt is similar to the JavaScript task runner, which you can use to automate your process. Webpack is a JavaScript module bundler that creates static assets from your dependencies. create-react-app, which we used in previous chapters, actually uses Webpack under the hood.

Security

You have to know the basics of web security and how to take care of these issues in web development. A good way to start learning is to read *OWASP Top 10 Most Critical Web Application Security Risks* (`https://www.owasp.org/index.php/Category:OWASP_Top_Ten_Project`). Then you have to learn how to handle these issues with the frameworks you are using.

Best practices

Software development is always team work and therefore it is really important that everyone in a team is using common best practices. Here, we will go through some basic things that you have to take into account. This is not the whole list, but we try to concentrate on some basic things that you should know.

Coding conventions

Coding conventions are guidelines that describe how the code should be written in a specific programming language. It makes code more readable and easier to maintain. Naming conventions define how variables, methods, and more should be named. Naming is really important because that helps developers understand the purpose of a certain unit in the program. The layout convention defines how the structure of the source code should look, for example, indenting and usage of spaces. The commenting convention defines how the source code should be commented. Quite often it is good to use some standardized ways for the commenting, such as Javadoc with Java.

Most of the software development environments and editors offer tools that help you with code conventions. You can also use code formatters, such as prettier for JavaScript.

Choosing the proper tools

You should always choose the proper tools that best fit your software development process. This makes your process more efficient and also helps you in the development life cycle. There are many tools to automate tasks in the development process and that is good way to avoid mistakes that occurs in repetitive tasks. Of course, the tools you use will depend on the process and the technologies you're using.

Choosing the proper technologies

When starting to develop an application, one of the first things to decide is which technologies (programming language, frameworks, databases, and so on) you should use. Quite often, it feels safe to select technologies that you have always used, but that's not always the optimal choice. The application itself normally makes some limitations to the technologies that you can use. For example, if you have to create a mobile application, there are several technologies that you can use. But if you have to develop a similar application that you have made many times, it might be wiser to use technologies that you already know well.

Minimizing the amount of coding

A common good practice is to minimize the amount of coding. This is really wise because it makes code maintenance and testing much easier. **DRY (Don't Repeat Yourself)** is a common principle in software development. The basic idea of DRY is to reduce the amount of code by avoiding repetitions in the code. It is always good practice to split your source code into smaller components because smaller units are always easier to manage. Of course, the optimum structure depends on the programming language you are using. One good statement is also **Keep it Simple, Stupid (KISS)** that should guide you in the right direction.

Summary

In this chapter, we covered the technologies that you should be familiar with if you want to become a full stack developer. The amount of knowledge that you should have sounds like a lot, but you don't have to be the master of all the technologies that we described. It is also good to understand some best practices of software development because then you can avoid common mistakes and your source code will be more readable and easier to maintain.

Questions

1. Why are coding conventions important?
2. Why should you try to avoid excessive coding?
3. Why are naming conventions important?

Further reading

Packt has other great resources for learning about full stack development:

- https://www.packtpub.com/application-development/complete-javascript-developer-primer-full-stack-js-video
- https://www.packtpub.com/application-development/full-stack-development-jhipster
- https://www.packtpub.com/networking-and-servers/fundamentals-continuous-delivery-pipeline-video

Assessments

Chapter 1

Answer 1: Spring Boot is Java-based web application framework that is based on Spring. With Spring Boot you can develop stand-alone web applications with embedded application server.

Answer 2: Eclipse is open source **integrated development environment (IDE)** and it is mostly used for Java programming, but it supports multiple other programming languages as well.

Answer 3: Maven is open source software project management tool. Maven can manage builds, documentation, testing, and more in the software development project.

Answer 4: The easiest way to start a new Spring Boot project is to create it with Spring Initializr web page. That creates a skeleton for your project with the modules that you need.

Answer 5: If you are using the Eclipse IDE you just activate you main class and press **Run** button. You can also use Maven command `mvn spring-boot:run` to run an application.

Answer 6: Spring Boot starter package provides logging features for you. You can define the level of logging in the `application.properties` settings file.

Answer 7: The error and log messages can be seen in the Eclipse IDE console after you run the application.

Chapter 2

Answer 1: ORM is a technique that allows you to fetch and manipulate from a database using an object-oriented programming paradigm. JPA provides object-relational mapping for Java developers. Hibernate is Java-based JPA implementation.

Answer 2: Entity class is just standard java class that is annotated with the `@Entity` annotation. Inside the class you have to implement constructors, fields, getters and setters. The field(s) that will be the unique id is annotated with the `@Id` annotation.

Answer 3: You have to create a new interface that extends Spring Data `CrudRepository` interface. In the type arguments you define the entity and the type of the `id` field, for example, `<Car, Long>`.

Answer 4: `CrudRepository` provides all CRUD operations to your entity. You can create, read, update, and delete your entities using the `CrudRepository`.

Answer 5: You have to create entity classes and link the entities using the `@OneToMany` and the `@ManyToOne` annotations.

Answer 6: You can add demo data in your main application class using `CommandLineRunner`.

Answer 7: Define the endpoint for the H2 console in your `application.properties` file and enable it. Then you can access the H2 console by navigating to the defined endpoint with a web browser.

Answer 8: You have to add MariaDB dependency to the `pom.xml` file and define the database connection settings in the `application.properties` file. Remove the H2 database dependency from the `pom.xml` file, if you have used that.

Chapter 3

Answer 1: REST is an architectural style for creating web services and it defines a set of constraints.

Answer 2: The easiest way to create RESTful web service with Spring Boot is to use Spring Data REST starter package. By default, the Spring Data REST finds all public repositories and creates automatically RESTful Web Services for your entities.

Answer 3: By sending a `GET` request to the endpoint of the entity. For example, if you have entity class called `Car` the Spring Data REST creates the endpoint called `/cars` that can be used to fetch all cars.

Answer 4: By sending a `DELETE` request to the endpoint of the individual entity item. For example, `/cars/1` deletes an car with id 1.

Answer 5: By sending a `POST` request to the endpoint of the entity. The header must contain the `Content-Type` field with the value `application/json` and the new item will be embedded in the request body.

Answer 6: By sending a PATCH request to the endpoint of the entity. The header must contain the Content-Type field with the value application/json and the updated item will be embedded in the request body.

Answer 7: You have to annotate your repository using the @RepositoryRestResource annotation. The query parameters are annotated using the @Param annotation.

Chapter 4

Answer 1: Spring Security provides security services for Java-based web applications.

Answer 2: You have to add Spring Security started package dependency to your pom.xml file. You can configure Spring Security by creating a security configuration class.

Answer 3: **JWT (JSON Web Token)** is a compact way to implement authentication in modern web applications. The size of the token is small and therefore it can be sent in the URL, in the POST parameter or inside the header.

Answer 4: You can use the Java JWT library that is the JSON web Token library for Java. The authentication service class adds and reads the token. The filter classes handles the login and authentication process.

Answer 5: You have to add Spring Boot test starter package to your pom.xml file. Spring Boot test starter package provides a lot of nice testing utilities, for example JUnit, AssertJ, and Mockito. When using the JUnit, the basic test classes are annotated with the @SpringBootTest annotation and the test methods should start with @Test annotation.

Answer 6: The test cases can be easily executed with the Eclipse IDE by running the test classes (**Run | JUnit test**). The test results can be seen in the **JUnit** tab.

Chapter 5

Answer 1: Node.js is an open source JavaScript-based server side environment. Npm is a package manager for JavaScript.

Answer 2: You can find the installation packages and instructions for multiple operating systems from https://nodejs.org/en/download.

Answer 3: **Visual Studio Code (VSCode)** is an open source code editor for multiple programming languages.

Answer 4: You can find the installation packages and instructions for multiple operating systems from `https://code.visualstudio.com`.

Answer 5: You have to install `create-react-app` globally using the npm. Then you create an app using the following command `create-react-app projectname`.

Answer 6: You can run the app using the following command `npm start` or `yarn start`.

Answer 7: You can start by modifying the `App.js` file and when you save the modification, you can see the changes immediately in the web browser.

Chapter 6

Answer 1: The components are the basic building blocks of the React apps. The React component can be created using a JavaScript function or ES6 class.

Answer 2: The props and state are the input data for rendering the component. They are JavaScript objects and the component is re-rendered when the props or the state are changing.

Answer 3: The data flow is going from the parent component to child.

Answer 4: The components that have only props are called stateless components. The components that have both the props and the state are called stateful components.

Answer 5: JSX is the syntax extension for JavaScript and it is recommended to use with React.

Answer 6: The component life cycle methods are executed at the certain phases of the component's life cycle.

Answer 7: It is similar to handling DOM element events. The difference in React is that event naming uses camelCase naming convention for example, `onClick` or `onSubmit` .

Answer 8: The common case is that we want to invoke a JavaScript function that has access to form data after the form submission. Therefore we have to disable default behavior using `preventDefault()` function. You can use input field's `onChange` event handler to save the values from a input fields to the state.

Chapter 7

Answer 1: A promise is an object the represents the result of an asynchronous operation. The use of promises simplifies the code when doing asynchronous calls.

Answer 2: The Fetch API provides `fetch()` method that you can use to make asynchronous calls using the JavaScript.

Answer 3: The REST API `fetch()` call is recommended to do inside the `componentDidMount()` life cycle method that is invoked when the component has been mounted.

Answer 4: You can access the response data using the promises with the `fetch()` method. The data from the response is saved to the state and the component is re-rendered when the state has changed.

Chapter 8

Answer 1: You can find the React component from multiple sources for example, `https://js.coach/` or `https://github.com/brillout/awesome-react-components`.

Answer 2: You can install React components using the npm or yarn package managers. When using npm, here is the command we use, `npm install <componentname>`.

Answer 3: You have to install React Table component. After the installation you can use the `ReactTable` component in the `render()` method. You have to define the data and the columns using the `ReactTable` props. The data can be an object or an array.

Answer 4: One way to create modal forms in React app is to use React Skylight component (`https://marcio.github.io/react-skylight/`).

Answer 5: You have to install Material-UI component library using the following command `npm install @material-ui/core`. After the library installation you can start to use components. The documentation of the different components can be found from `https://material-ui.com`.

Answer 6: Routing can be implemented using the React Router component (`https://github.com/ReactTraining/react-router`).

Chapter 9

Answer 1: With the mock-up, it is much easier to discuss needs with the client before you start to write any actual code. Changes to the mock-up are really easy and fast to do, compared to modifications with real frontend source code.

Answer 2: There is lot of suitable applications available to do mock-ups easily. You can also use paper and pencil to create mock-up.

Answer 3: You can modify the security configuration class to allow access to all endpoints without authentication.

Chapter 10

Answer 1: First you have to call REST API using the `fetch()` method. Then, you can access the response data using the promises with the `fetch()` method. The data from the response is saved to the state and the component is re-rendered when the state has changed.

Answer 2: You have to send a `DELETE` method request using the `fetch()` method. The endpoint of the call is the link to the item that you want to delete.

Answer 3: You have to send a `POST` method request using the `fetch()` method to the entity endpoint. The added item should be embedded in the body and you have to add `Content-Type` header with `application/json` value.

Answer 4: You have to send a `PATCH` method request using the `fetch()` method. The endpoint of the call is the link to the item that you want to update. The updated item should be embedded in the body and you have to add `Content-Type` header with `application/json` value.

Answer 5: You can use some third-party React component to show toast messages like React Toastify.

Answer 6: You can use some 3rd party React component to export data to CSV file like React CSV.

Chapter 11

Answer 1: Material-UI is the component library for React and it implement the Google's Material Design.

Answer 2: First you have to install Material-UI library using the following command `npm install @material-ui/core`. Then you can start to use component from the library. The documentation of the different components can be found from `https://material-ui.com/`.

Answer 3: You can remove a component using the following npm command `npm remove <componentname>`.

Chapter 12

Answer 1: Jest is a test library for JavaScript and it is developed by Facebook.

Answer 2: Create a test file using the `.test.js` extension. Implement your test cases inside the file and you can run the tests using the following command `npm test`.

Answer 3: For the snapshot testing you have to install `react-test-render` package and you have to import `renderer` to you test file. Implement your snapshot test cases inside the file and you can run the tests using the following command `npm test`.

Answer 4: Enzyme is a JavaScript library for testing the React component's output.

Answer 5: Using the following npm command `npm install enzyme enzyme-adapter-react-16 --save-dev`.

Answer 6: You have to import `Enzyme` and `Adapter` components to your test file. Then you can create you test cases to render a component. With the Enzyme, you can use Jest for assertions.

Answer 7: Enzyme provides the `simulate` method that can be used to test events.

Chapter 13

Answer 1: You have to create a new component that renders input fields for the username and the password. The component contains also a button that calls /login endpoint when the button is pressed.

Answer 2: The call from the login component is made using the POST method and an user object is embedded in the body. If the authentication is succeeded, the backend sends the token back in the Authorization header.

Answer 3: The token can be saved to session storage using the sessionStorage.setItem() method.

Answer 4: The token have to be included to the request's Authorization header.

Chapter 14

Answer 1: You can create an executable JAR file by using the following Maven command mvn clean install.

Answer 2: The easiest way to deploy Spring Boot application is to push your application source code to the GitHub and use GitHub link from the Heroku.

Answer 3: The easiest way to deploy the React app to Heroku is to use the Heroku Buildpack for create-react-app (https://github.com/mars/create-react-app-buildpack).

Answer 4: Docker is a container platform that makes software development, deployment, and shipping easier. Containers are lightweight and executable software packages that include everything that is needed to run software.

Answer 5: The Spring Boot application is just an executable JAR file that can be executed with Java. Therefore, you can create Docker container for Spring Boot application similar way than you create for any Java JAR application.

Answer 6: You can pull the latest MariaDB container from the Docker Hub using the following Docker command docker pull mariadb:latest.

Chapter 15

Answer 1: It makes code more readable and easier to maintain. It also makes team work much easier because everyone are using the same structure in the coding.

Answer 2: It makes code more readable and easier to maintain. The testing of the code is easier.

Answer 3: It makes code more readable and easier to maintain. It also makes team work much easier because everyone are using the same naming convention in the coding.

Other Books You May Enjoy

If you enjoyed this book, you may be interested in these other books by Packt:

Hands-On High Performance with Spring 5
Chintan Mehta, Subhash Shah, Pritesh Shah, Prashant Goswami, Dinesh Radadiya

ISBN: 978-1-78883-838-2

- Master programming best practices and performance improvement with bean wiring
- Analyze the performance of various AOP implementations
- Explore database interactions with Spring to optimize design and configuration
- Solve Hibernate performance issues and traps
- Leverage multithreading and concurrent programming to improve application performance
- Gain a solid foundation in JVM performance tuning using various tools
- Learn the key concepts of the microservice architecture and how to monitor them
- Perform Spring Boot performance tuning, monitoring, and health checks

Building RESTful Web Services with Spring 5 - Second Edition
Raja CSP Raman, Ludovic Dewailly

ISBN: 978-1-78847-589-1

- Deep dive into the principles behind REST
- Expose CRUD operations through RESTful endpoints with the Spring Framework
- Devise response formats and error handling strategies, offering a consistent and flexible structure to simplify integration for service consumers
- Follow the best approaches for dealing with a service's evolution while maintaining backward compatibility
- Understand techniques to secure web services
- Comply with the best ways to test RESTful web services, including tips for load testing
- Optimise and scale web services using techniques such as caching and clustering

Leave a review - let other readers know what you think

Please share your thoughts on this book with others by leaving a review on the site that you bought it from. If you purchased the book from Amazon, please leave us an honest review on this book's Amazon page. This is vital so that other potential readers can see and use your unbiased opinion to make purchasing decisions, we can understand what our customers think about our products, and our authors can see your feedback on the title that they have worked with Packt to create. It will only take a few minutes of your time, but is valuable to other potential customers, our authors, and Packt. Thank you!

Index

A

add functionality 193, 194, 196, 197
AppBar component
  using 214
asynchronous operation
  promise state 132
  using 131
Awesome React Components
  reference link 149

B

backend programming language 266
backend
  deploying 248, 249, 250, 252, 253, 254, 256
Button component
  using 208, 209

C

CORS (Cross Origin Resource Sharing) 89
create-react-app
  reference link 103
CRUD functionalities
  add functionality 193, 194, 196, 197
  delete functionality 186, 187, 188, 190, 191, 192
  edit functionality 198, 201, 202
  list page, creating 179, 180, 182, 183, 186
  other functionalities 203
CRUD repositories
  creating 35, 36, 38
CSS 266

D

Database as a Service (DBaaS) 252
databases 267

delete functionality 186, 187, 188, 190, 191, 192
Docker container
  using 258, 260, 261, 262
DRY (Don't Repeat Yourself) 269

E

Eclipse
  basics 8
  installing 8
  URL 8
edit functionality 198, 201, 202
entity classes
  creating 26, 28, 30, 32, 34
Enzyme
  using 227, 228
ES6 (ECMAScript 2015) 114
ES6
  arrow functions 115
  basics 114
  classes 116
  constants 114
  inheritance 116
  styling 117
  template literals 116

F

Fetch API
  using 133
frontend frameworks 267
frontend libraries 267
frontend
  deploying 256
full-stack developer
  backend programming language 266
  CSS 266
  databases 267

frontend frameworks 267
frontend libraries 267
HTML 266
HTTP 266
JavaScript 266
learning 265
tools 267
version control 267
web security 267

G

Grid component
  using 211

H

HAL (Hypertext Application Language) 61
hibernate 26
HTML 266
HTTP 266

J

Java JWT library
  reference link 83
Java Persistent API (JPA)
  about 26
  basics 26
JavaScript 266
Jest
  using 222, 223
JS.coach
  URL 148
JSON Web Tokens (JWT) 82
JWT authentication
  used, for securing backend 232
  used, for securing frontend 233, 235, 236, 238,
    239, 240, 242, 243

L

list page
  creating 179, 180, 182, 183, 186
Long-term Support (LTS) 100

M

MariaDB database
  setting up 48, 49
MariaDB
  installing 21, 22
  URL 21
  URL, for installation 25
Material UI component library 162, 163, 165
Maven
  basics 8
modal window component 158, 161

N

Node.js
  installing 100

O

Object-Relational Mapping (ORM)
  about 26
  basics 26
OpenWeatherMap
  URL 135

P

PaaS (Platform as a Service) 247
project object model (pom) 9

R

React app
  creating 103
  Enzyme, using 227, 228
  executing 103
  Jest, using 222, 223
  modifying 105, 106
  snapshot testing 224, 225, 227
React Material-UI
  AppBar component, using 214
  Button component, using 208, 209
  Grid component, using 211
  SnackBar component, using 216, 217
  TextField component, using 212
React project
  creating, for frontend 175

React Router
  reference link 165
React Table
  about 153, 154, 157
  URL 153
React
  component life cycle methods 121
  components 109, 111, 112, 113
  ES6, basics 114
  events, handling with 124
  forms, handling with 125, 126, 128
  JSX 117
  lists, handling with 122, 123
  props and state 118, 119
  technical requisites 109
REST (Representational State Transfer)
  about 54
  basics 54
  cacheable 54
  client server 54
  code on demand 54
  layered system 54
  stateless 54
  uniform interface 54
REST APIs
  examples 135, 136, 138, 140, 142
REST architecture
  Hypermedia and the Engine of Application State
   (HATEOAS) 54
  resource manipulation, through representation
   54
  resources, identification 54
  self descriptive messages 54
RESTful web service
  creating 55, 57, 59, 60
  creating, with Spring Boot 53
routing 165, 167

S

SnackBar component
  using 216, 217
snapshot testing 224, 225, 227
software development
  best practices 268
  coding conventions 268

coding, minimization 269
  technologies, selecting 269
  tools, selecting 268
Spring Boot applications
  environment, setting up 7
  tools, setting up 7
Spring Boot backend
  preparing 173
Spring Boot development tools 18
Spring Data REST
  using 61, 62, 64, 65, 68
Spring Initializr
  project, creating with 10
Spring Security
  about 71, 73, 74, 77, 78, 79, 81
  backend securing, JWT used 82, 85, 87, 89, 90
  features 72
  Spring Boot, testing 91
  unit tests, creating 92, 93, 95
  URL 71
Spring Tool Suite (STS) 9
stateful components 120
stateless components 120

T

tables
  relationships between 40, 42, 44, 46
TextField component
  using 212
third-party React components
  using 148, 151
tools 267
tools, Spring Boot applications
  Eclipse, basics 8
  Eclipse, installing 8
  logs and problem, solving 18, 20
  MariaDB, installing 21, 22
  Maven, basics 8
  project, creating with Spring Initializr 10
  project, executing 12, 13, 14, 16, 17
  Spring Boot development tools 18

U

user interface

mocking up 172

V

version control 267
Visual Studio Code (VS Code)
  about 101
  installing 101, 102
  URL, for downloading 101

W

web security 267